My God... The Dance...

Other books by the author include

DEW POINT *forthcoming*
BOOK PARADISE: SPILLIKINS
LIKE THOSE OF AN EERIE RUIN
THE MAKING OF A STORY
LITHOS
collected to 2012 POEMS &
TRANSLATIONS *collected to 2012*
TRANSLATIONS ADDENDA *to 2023*
ANTONYMS ANEW: BARBS & LOVES
InExperience and UnCommon Sense in Translation
OSIP MANDELSTAM: WHOEVER HAS FOUND A HORSESHOE
ELSA MORANTE: ALIBI

LISTENING FOR HENRY CROWDER
UnNatural Music
DESERT SANDS: STUFF SMITH
BLACK GYPSY: EDDIE SOUTH
FALLEN FROM THE MOON: JUICE WILSON
POEM ABOUT MUSIC

THE LITERATURE DIRECTOR *a play in one act online at*
https://fortnightlyreview.co.uk/2023/03/barnett-lit-director/

SNOW LIT REV, ED.

Anthony Barnett

My God, You Have a Lot to Answer for, But You Won't, Will You: Sing Songs

preceded by

The Dance Is Not Believable

A·B

My God . . . The Dance . . .
Copyright © Anthony Barnett 2025

Anthony Barnett is hereby identified
as the moral rights author of this work

All rights reserved

reprinting or online posting or scanning for
that purpose in whole or in part without
the written permission of the copyright
holder is prohibited except as allowed
in fair use in such as a review

Acknowledgements, sources, explications
are given on the last pages

Typeset in Centaur MT with four
Cyrillic glyphs in after-Centaur Coelacanth
by AB©omposer

Printed by TJ Books Padstow

First published 2025 by
Allardyce Book ABP
14 Mount Street · Lewes · East Sussex BN7 1HL UK
www.abar.net

CIP record for this book is
available from The British Library

ISBN 978-0-907954-80-4

*As-tu foi
comme il enroule au mot,*
—Édouard Glissant

*Par exemple, il lui fait chanter des chansons dont il n'écoute pas les paroles,
mais dont la musique accompagne les visions de son monde caché.*
—Valéry Larbaud, *Enfantines*

blah blah blah
—Greta Thunberg

voice your dignity in this final flight . . .
—Kiuchi Kumiko

*Ma la mia mente fallisce e non parlo
non parlo a nessuno.*
—Andrea Zanzotto

THE DANCE...

2022

The sentence in German in the penultimate passage is spoken by Mephisto in Else Lasker-Schüler's play *IchundIch* written in Jerusalem in the 1940s, her last place of exile because Switzerland would not take her back following a visit

The dance is not believable. Not unbelievable but not believable. The
 applause is audible not yet plausible. A lifetime of dust
 accumulated through both long- and short-sightedness. I do not
 believe I need your book any longer, if I ever did. Yes I did. O
 horrible horrible new and old news. Disgrace of the
 ineffectuality.

You have listened to the no-longer abundant regent honeyeater losing its
 song, picking up instead songs of the more prolific species
 surrounding it. Because birds mimic.

A disturbance in the grass which is not the wind. Sprouting sports of
 little concern. The world could care less about your dispersed
 formlessness. Infliction not inflection of uncarried voices.

Shall you no longer learn how to spell? To enter into a realm of detritus
 left right behind. Blocked by adventurousness. To enter into
 others' lives, derelict once used up. A dog appears, to inquire, to
 greet. So many dogs, some friendly, some not so friendly.
 Despairing at the script. Do you know some thing is wrong
 dreadful whirling helicopter? Unreasonable irrational uninspired
 bird.

You will not respond. I swear. How I swear. What truthfulness is there
 in the echelons of what you think is your elegant written
 ecstasy? How deflated! Shall I deprive-deprave you? How can I?
 I have nothing important to fight against. Shame.

Remembrance of shame. Misspelt spent self. Must I read your poetry
 again, escaping an inviolable space? I lunge lash lunch. See what
 you look like! Do not lean back too quickly because you might
 choke on the almonds.

[9]

Diffuse. Do not raise your eyebrows to the heavens. They cannot help you. I am lost on you. Those ladies are more than adventurous. So relive and release your performances.

Do you claim idiocy? You can laugh. Can you? In your supercharge. To buy a pineapple, however small, from a far part of the world for a mere £1. What sense? If I sleep on my left side my left arm aches. If I sleep on my right side my right rump aches. Exposed roots steps. What sense? In vain I look for our names in the indexes of books written before us. So I stick out my feet when seated on a public garden bench so that passersby on the path are obliged to keep their distance in the plague year. Of course I tuck them in for a buggy or a toddler.

Pumice stone, a large piece, brought back from a beach in the Arctic Circle. Wrong assertions. Wrong notations. We can tell the photo was taken on a boat, a packet steamer to be precise, in the evening, or at night, in the summer of 1928.

I act myself. I counteract. I knock the sense out of me. Once I was lost on you. Emerge from the sun. Acknowledge exceptions. Look —obedience is it?—at the behaviour of the trees. Remember?— to forget? Inconceivably harsh words and swipes. Think of that inconceivable rewritten novel. Fitful befitting nonsense.

Sea is not to your liking. A lake, an inland sea, is to your liking. Your pen seems to have a will of its own. You look around in disparate desperate bewilderment. Does it? Your wonder words are not wonderful. You? Wandering. Indecipherable gibberish. And still you wonder if what you would like will appear.

There. You go again. Wandering forms of beauty. What is your
 principle? Biting. Put away the notebook. Things are not as
 dark as you think.

Break like the sea. The sea that is not for you. With big and little toes
 turned inwards.

I come back to your rotten countries. Not everything is rotten. The
 middle letter is too insignificant.

Who is it who approaches stealthily? Opened. After all, what else is
 there for you to do? Do you tire of your tongue? Yes, I do.
 Then understand the citrus. Disembodied. I believe it is
 whelmed. May your lithium cell if not your voice wear out.
 Then you will be quiet.

I arrive as if from afar with teeth on edge. Espalier. Or it is in memory
 of frozen lakes that the glyphs are let out. So I ask for a
 different tongue. It is not the fault of Mother Nature that they
 are let out.

Music has begun to disturb. Incomprehensible. Deliberations. How
 different things could have been. Searching for your unjustifed
 speechlessness. Protection of different types of troublesome
 amateurs. I-You have a lot to answer for. Oh, yes, as you grow
 older de jure de facto.

Are you flirting with the impossible? Across the seas? Why is your walk
 unlike anyone or everyone else's? Are you planning to walk on
 water, with a touch of paranoia? At the obsolescent circus a
 tightrope walker.

Your hair cut short or allowed to grow long. What does it matter? What difference does it make? To either of them? And now a lawyer appears in last night's dream. Why? She says yes to an invitation to dinner. Where is the restaurant? A little more happened but I think it best to keep silent. In these tumultuous days without privacy.

Run a mile. Easy. O, that you allow iniquities. How you love to look as if you are doing something. Eruptions. This is your detritus. Left to breathe, it hardly matters what you write. If you scan me. If you cross the expanse. If you pile it on. Run after your own. What deciduous decision making. And your what have yous. What do you turn into with such long legs? Metabolism. Ownership. You doggone fonts. With a heavy heart and head. Quite. Often.

Where thumbnail and thumb meet. Steady the rock. Stop the forces of this or that toppling and crashing into the froth. Bare your forehead beforehand. Laugh. Act out what you take to be yours. Perpitude. Oh, look, the first pages of the notebook have not been used. I mean, the pages have been used but what is written on them has not.

I no longer like my script. The mound that is your tummy. The sun does not allow the colour red to compete with itself. I can only assume the opaqueness of your own dream. Cuttlefish. Out of my mind? While a dream in the past occurs in a new dream. One fantasy wins over another.

Broken voice. You forget how to scream, how to construct a myth out of the inexplicable. You would like to open a word between your fingers and your thumb as you would a fig.

Staggered by the well. By the indirection of the breeze. Of course I am a philosopher. But not as you know them. An uninformed philosopher, tired of his tongue. Very tired. I can look for your name in the indexes to very old books.

We are to grow unsteady on our feet in search of reasons. Equally at work over bare earth and blank paper. Reasons to combat the unbearable stench of the politics in the fault of impermanent perceptions. Do you have a choice? Not a chance.

Take care of the labels. An irritation moves from one site to another. First an arm. Then a rib. Then a leg. Then the back of the neck. Then the shoulder blade.

The bivalve's silent scream. St Anthony's kiss of tongues. An afternoon tea. I intertwine my fingers with the right hand's thumb over the left. I bury my head, not only in the sand. And there the music is quite beautiful again.

He is seen in the streets by himself—by himself?—he himself sees himself?—beside himself—blaspheming, mutters, occasional shouts, idiots idiots. At home his shouts are more like howls. He himself is an idiot.

Nerve never-endings. What do you mean? In your stupidity your ignorance paint a kitchen with a watercolour. In. Leave alone aforehead.

I keep biting my tongue, my lip, but not to keep quiet, and my cheek. It may happen when I eat certain things, an apple, for example. I am not myself. I must swear only under my breath.

Who wears their big sunglasses in their head of hair. The answer, if it is a question, is known but it is not a question. It is a statement.

How is it that hell in that tongue is bright? O, it is the fire. It is difficult for my tongue to say langu'. Usurped by confidence poets.

Always into the mountains. There goes Jakob. There goes Georg. There goes Franz. There goes Paul. And there goes Robert. Others too. There I walked. Familiar, Unfamiliar. Not always I.

She exudes embarrassed cookiness. So coy. And at his cocky strut and swagger my appetite is losing me.

What is long drawn out has the look of a question but it is not one. What I am allowed to talk about within your sphere. Without recourse to a score. Whoops of delight from an audience. Herald trumpet.

The name of the flower is forgotten for the moment. A colour for your eye.

I did not say there was a problem. Appropriate word. Leaf lips. Who are you? Why are you wearing black? I remember I have forgotten.

Ay Aya. Six months in the State of Palestine. I shall call it that. Aye amidst confusion. I. Thee. Eyes.

Scatter your light. *Wär Gott nicht »Gott« verlör Er den Verstand!*

Dance.

MY GOD...

c.2017–2024 if not timeless

✦ ✦ ✦

I do not question you. Heavens, no! I would rather say Heaven. There you are. I shall do my best to ignore you. Sing songs prove it. Suffering encourages all to suffer some children pick the poppy heads. Religious intolerance apoplexy. Yet drink has not yet taken to me. What will the child say as she is growing? You fumble with your tote trouble is too much and the man and the woman sigh within themselves and outside of themselves, noman or yeoman and woeman he undoffs his hat in recognition of her headscarf daisies daisy chain who startled her legs become parts of poems.

And the heart gives out, not always. Linguistic kisses. Playful chalk marks of the children on the paving stones

What does an ant want on the arm of a garden bench then on the arm

The miracle of male and female and the last day of sun before days of rain. Dead mask death mask

I close my eyes
to what
Yet I watch
I unplait garlic bulbs
Do I forever write
I have given myself over
to what

The flower leaf
Over
I star myself
I cross myself
I star myself

O ceremonial sward
Whose crown do you crop

O ceremonial walk

Search for yourself

How pleasing it is to listen to the foreign words one does not understand. They waft with their music. How pleasing it is to read a book one likes or at least may learn, or otherwise, from. What is it goes on in a bird's head imitating human speech? Giants? Captain Quickshot set sail for the offshore windfarm. Riveting. Won over? Once upon a space-time continuum . . . Wait a moment let me gather up my momentous thoughts.

Discourse in their beauty in this world. All the mighty are fallen from plinths. A pride of big cats. If you come increasingly to a supposition that Latin script is not quite all there. I can swear with the best of them but I shall try not to.

She says, I have little sea shoes, which is a delight, on the seashore, off course.

Overleaf. So. I mean. What do I mean? Do you know what is carried within you? O small largesse known as smalless. Do not accept anything other than large largesse. Do not demean devalue undermine.

Whatever.

Ask not for the day to come quicker it shall shorten life.

Applause. Is it not a curious thing this clapping of hands or its absence. And the ears. They are curious. Applause should have an essay.

Imaginable imarginal magical

Tired reading exhausted like doing something else

Bumblebee climbing a grass stalks but it always bend over under its weight at the top on its last legs gave it a clover it wasn't, wasn't able to be, interested

Disappeared into the distance

Is it perhaps not that the person commits but that the swirling water or the fuming exhaust draws in.

Bare and born in my skin. What is it like? But you cannot can you

O the matter-master. What is it? Hiding in a corner of lost last loss-ingness.

Is the whole history of music one long work-in-progress?

Noises off

I'm certainly not Walser but I can still write about "Little Town Scenes". Later. For they occur

Pornography is really very understandable but it is also really very silly

Big toe what of it? I was going to say but no. In a little because of foolish childhood shoes

You know you have a charming way about you. Your little to and fro dance almost imperceptible but perceptible sway when you smile and talk

With what indignation this elegant willowy goth or was it she replied when he asked her to confirm "are you in the queue" because it was not clear that she was or it was

Keep your distance or die laughter

Buzzy busy bees

Commencements

Writers artists madness of difference consciousness

What voice do I have

At an angle seat seated

in a cooling breeze
not freezing
confronting a wicket gate in silex
pretty and nervous

Reader, you may be forgiven for thinking the subtitle of this work is drawn from Larbaud, for example. It is not. I came across the following sentence while rereading *Childish Things,* translated by Catherine Wald, months after settling on both title and subtitle.

> *For example, he has her sing songs whose words he doesn't listen to, but whose music accompanies the visions of his hidden world.*

Which is a proper translation—see the epigraph. What is more *Sing Songs* was at one time thought not to be the subtitle but the title.

Takashi-san, I would like to write about a walnut, a wild hard to crack mountain walnut. I have a handful but I think I cannot.

You are beside yourself with creaking branches in the wind thought for a moment to be talk.

Wrist. Stirrings. What stirrings? Resort to the pen in touch with the world. Why? Why do you ask? Is it too difficult? Symphony sympathy.

And at that there is an old notice, not to be taken too much notice of, with a pinch of salt and a something-or-other, a dollop, of honey.

You are your touchstone
You are my touchstone
Touchstone

Again, I can but name you now hound and then all then it has been evermore picked off many by many silent anguished disturbance.

So let your disgust wash over you cleansing you without much punctuation to speak of perhaps a period or two. Why? For your want of something different, of course. Float over you would be better.

        Heavens above lies below
        One or another or is it both
        Puts on a good or bad show
        Either way it's nothing but froth

antirrhinum means false nose
as antirhythm arose
will do will not do

You cannot be heard
Good

Yeses and noes

A meaningless note

Yes, what is it we know, that you come in and talk about so glibly.

I made a note about what to write about but it is such a cryptic note I have hardly the faintest idea what it is supposed to be about. I had thought that jotting down just a word or two would be enough.

Who gives her all o withering look it is not some little bird rustling leaves beech nuts splitting and falling on my head be it should I stay sitting on a bench

Oh I am tired, tired of your concerns your cinema, gestures of futility and yet and yet you have poured yourself an unusual drop

It does not make sense.

Almighty puny power. You have it yet you do not.

It is not your salt it is my salt my snow my sand, so sayeth the Lord because if you do not already know it it is also not only without but with that anything is possible. Now will you misconstrue

I bury my head in my pillow not in your sand. I have remembered to remember. Long ago I pummelled pillows into a pillow book but I wonder and abutt this living in a past

flagonship of grapes

HAVE A HEART

Once there was a boy who had difficulty holding on to his heart. If he did not score well at some sport he lost heart. If he could not solve a mathematical problem or write an interesting line for his essay or figure out the fingering on his musical instruments he lost heart. It really did not matter what he put his mind to, he lost heart. He managed to pick his heart, that is, himself, up by himself after every disappointment until the day he lost his heart to a girl. She hardly noticed him. Skipping and jumping about she narrowly avoided stepping on a heart right there in front of her on the path. "Goodness, what are you doing there all by yourself?" "A boy lost me. The boy over there under the tree in a scene from an idyll trying to write poems, looking a bit sheepish, I'd say." The girl gathered up the heart. She gave the boy back his heart, Or, "I'm heartless. I couldn't care less." She gave the heart a flying kick. The heart landed on the boy's lap. "Do you like Silvina Ocampo's stories?" "Yes, I do." Whichever it might have been, when they came of age they married. They had lots of children.

If only I had learned to laugh then as I do now, even in insolence.

God forsaken lamb I wish I knew what to think I mean what do I think.

I wonder at what the insect is doing here even if I understand I do not understand.

Shaking like a coffee leaf so many stories to tell but I do not know if I can.

How often must you rummage in your bag, your box of tricks?

I left with a sour taste in my mouth. I had been talking with myself, I think it was myself. At least I was talking with and not to. I rid myself of my jumper. Good riddance. The next moment a cloud covered the sun. One might say it came over me. Should I be satisfied with my stupidity?

It is nothing but sticks

A goalie looks on feigning futility and the air is punched. How could you ever imagine. No nothing new except I spy a microdot in i

Plants are not like that in a confident young stride. Oh gosh what strangeness what stratagems what strange people including myself of course a moment's heat

"Your book will be big?" "of Biblical proportions."

Magical. What a word? What can you make it out to mean? Look the world in the eye. Those who do not see what they can get away with. You think you can fill up with poetrol here or gasolines there. Actually, you are not funny. Not at all.

To the flowers the very little boy says on his very little bicycle. No! the equally little girl says on her equally little bicycle, which she had earlier rammed into a flowering bush.

Flutter-flicker eyelids

You have the sweetest face

So different

Frighten me

Him who

Little conversations.

"TIME IS THIS PAPER ON WHICH I WRITE"

"let me take this opportunity to reaffirm that I am not writing a novel." H. (or ?) says in José Saramago's *Manual of Painting & Calligraphy*, which is the perfect translation of the Portuguese title. Was it the publisher (probably) or translator who added *: A Novel* presumably in an effort to disguise, distinguish it from, a "manual"? Apparently, Portuguese readers (of novels) mistook it for that when it first came out, so it flopped. Let us investigate, a little.

Rather arbitrarily I pick out from a stack on the shelf *Manual* to reread. I had fogotten my scrawled spidery black annotations with which I am now confronted on the flyleaf and opposite and inside, including the gist of what I have just asked.

"I am not myself unless my pen is travelling these pages like a ski stick across the snow." It is scrawled on the flyleaf without a usual page annotation. I am assuming it is a quotation. I cannot be sure unless I go through the book a third time. Did I write it? I can't believe it.

"Him that has ears to hear, let him hear." A quotation. Adapted because the translator has the grammar wrong. I used to and most do. Fascinating.

"And anyone who takes the trouble to study antiquity will discover that painting and sculpture were simply called painting and that in the time of Demosthenes they were called antigraphy, which means to draw or write, a term common to both of these sciences, so that the writings of Agatharcus may be referred to as the paintings of Agatharcus [*sic*]." I see.

"In my opinion, everything is biography. I insist with even greater reason, as someone in pursuit, that everything is autobiography (autobiography? reason?)." A round of applause for the parentheses.

"I would now have to discover write-painting, this latest and universal esperanto which will transform all of us into writer-painters and, with any luck, into practitioners of those blessed artemages." Picture postcards of paintings.

"I know a fair amount about painting and now know enough about calligraphy to perceive (and try to put into practice) that the expression of incoherence demands a great deal of organization. I am speaking of expression, not simply about revealing oneself." Oh.

"What finally resulted from this attempt to write an autobiography [. . .] combining fact and fiction in equal measure?" That's it.

"'one of these days I'll give you some papers of mine I'd like you to read.' 'Secrets?' she asked smiling. 'No. Just papers. Things I've written.'" Here endeth *Manual*.

✶

Make up your mind. If you think you are done, you are not.

Ends in self-portrait

Dispense with being hunted

Mosque is mask in absence

What is meant by the end of the garden

Flora is not like in a confident young stride

Oh such strangeness
such strange people
un-myself of course
a moment's heat

Would that I have been pleased to write this. All have stories so those autobiographies those biographies those memoirs are much less important than the mysteriousness of writing.

So many kisses

Oh lovely church bells
disturbing the peace
for the sake of
How peaceful when they stop their clamour
or delightful
O nonsense delightful

Awaitness. Tiresome voice "be quiet". Cut of the cloth. A vexatious vacancy tenacious and tiring

Oblique miserability. What brings you here? How do you see? How do you reveal yourself? I can draw upon you.

Reread—past tense—Akhmatova, Mandelstam, Tsvetaeva, especially essays, etc. Understand at least a little about Russia, god knows who or what. God? I was present when Akhmatova received her honorary degree. I thought it was Cambridge but no. It was Oxford. How curious a confusion, conflating two different occasions accompanying an editor to both. Cambridge was a visit to a modern languages scholar. I remember a room, dark in daylight, packed with bookshelves with scarcely enough space to squeeze between them. God knows how . . .

Am I impatient? I can't imagine it. I have waited eighty years to get to forty-one.

POETRY

New York-resident Mexican Valeria Luiselli's first books—a novel, a sequence of brief essays, a second novel—were written in Spanish before being translated into English. Now she writes directly in English: most of the docu-essay *Tell Me How It Ends* and all of the inextricably linked novel *Lost Children Archive*. I don't believe she has ever published poetry, at least not in English, but poets, mostly real, sometimes kind of imaginary, permeate her work.

If I mention her first novel, *Faces in the Crowd*, it is to show early proof of that: Gilberto Owen is a real Mexican poet, living in New York in 1928. Why should I expect Joshua Zvorsky to be a real poet too. I feel quite stupid checking out www to see if anything is posted there about him. I know perfectly well he is one of Valeria Luiselli's conceits. From the first mention of these faces in the crowd it is obvious that Zvorsky, author of *That*, translator of Owen, is Louis

Zukofsky. The more one enters the past and present obfuscations of this bonbon of a novel the clearer that, indeed all, becomes. The question I have to ask myself is why Zvorsky when all Owen, Williams, Dickinson, Pound, Lorca, Langston Hughes, half a dozen others, for example, Beckett, Wittgenstein, not to mention Duke Ellington, are checked with their real names even though their conversations, or the conversations about them, take place only in Luiselli's imagination. Thus, a thinly disguised Louis Zukofsky, Joshua Zvorsky, engages with Mexican poet Gilberto Owen and Federico García Lorca. The novel is alternately set in the present, in which Luiselli searches for traces of Owen, and 1928 Harlem, where Luiselli finds him, along with impossible glimpses of Pound. Owen, Zvorsky, Lorca visit a bar and floor show. Ellington is playing piano. Lorca brags "The Duke and I are big buddies." Which is about, I was about to say objective, as subjective as you can get.

Tell Me How It Ends is Luiselli's heart-rending, but also heart-warming, documentation of her work, partly personal, partly social and practical, partly academic, assisting Central American and Mexican migrant children in USA during the Obama administration, whose plight, as she knows in a postscript, has only grown worse post-Obama. A shorter version of the essay first appeared in the journal *Freeman's*, whose proprietor encouraged her to write it. "The stories told in this essay are true.", Luiselli writes, "All names of the children I have interviewed in court, as well as specific facts about their biographical information and that of their sponsers, have been changed in order to protect them."

"There are things that can only be understood retrospectively, when many years have passed and the story has ended. In the meantime, while the story continues, the only thing to do is tell it over and over again as it develops, bifurcates, knots around itself. And it must be told, because before anything can be understood, it has to be narrated many times, in many different words and from many different angles, by many different minds." True to her word, Luiselli retells the story, fictionalized, in *Lost Children Archive*, which includes a car with a set of boxes of tapes and documents, which become chapters. But there is a startling difference. The long road trip, retold in the novel, with her husband, with his son, her stepson, with her daughter, her husband's stepdaughter, none of them referred to by a name, carries with it the gradual, seemingly inevitable, break-up of the marriage. That doesn't happen in the earlier essay so we cannot be sure what really happened—it is a novel after all, or so we are more often than not led to believe—yet the grounding in inescapable facts is born out by numerous corrolations with the essay and by the inclusion of a set of polaroids illustrative of recounted events.

We find Luiselli's penchant for poetry asserting itself once again, not only in peppered references to and quotations from writers, including Pound, Eliot, Kinnell, Rilke, Anne Carson, but in a middle-of-the-night encounter in Dicks Whiskey Bar: "He says he used to be a photographer but now prefers painting, and is going to Poetry, Texas, because he's been commissioned to paint a series of portraits of the town's eldest generation." Incredulity is resolved a few pages later in the section "Guns & Poetry": "We go back to studying the map. [. . .] I follow the line of a highway with the tip of my index finger. I pass places like Hope, Pleasant, Commerce, de-route toward Merit, south to Fate, and then to Poetry, Texas, which, to my amazement, does indeed exist."

What of the "Lost Children"? They are both the migrants that wife and husband go in search of, inextricably entwined with wife's stepson, and with husband's very young stepdaughter who goes potentially dangerously walkabout in the night in seach of those migrant children. Caveat: there is something in the book that I cannot quite believe in. In later sections, the narrative is no longer voiced by the wife, the unnamed her, but by her stepson. It is a dislocation, which comes across as awkward, in a way that other dislocations (a most appropiate word), of which there are many, are not awkward, but innovatively fitting, in what is ultimately an extraordinary body of work—I hesitate to say novel—in which Poetry does indeed exist.

*

Oh yes, I was an actor. The King, a blackbird pie. And then in spring Professor Total Loss.

Oh for heaven's sake there is no place for the poem except in the poem.

MOSAIC

Calliope Michail's *Along Mosaic Roads* is a début chapbook from The 87 Press. What a wonderful début it is, both for Michail and for The 87. Michail's background is American and Greek. She grew up in Athens in a house of music: "the sweet plucking of the / baglama, the rumbling currents of the / cello—I trace my blood". She lives in London, where she had been studying. Described on the cover as "a series of lyrical peregrinations that chart journeys into the real and imagined spaces of wanderlust, desire, origins and memory"—I can hardly better those words—*Along Mosaic Roads* consists of five sections entitled "Standing on the Sun". The opening part-poem of each section is in italic. All except the last section have three more poems, with that central, italic, poem weaving through the whole.

It comes as a shock, on opening the book, to read a second epigraph from Charles Manson. It is not what one would expect. On reflection it is a not uninteresting, not entirely irrelevant, bitter quote (I'll put it that way) more or less about travelling getting one nowhere except where one is. In that, it is a rejoinder to the humane first epigraph from Walt Whitman: "You road I enter upon and look around, I believe you are not all that is here, I believe that much unseen is also here." This is true relevance to *Along Mosaic Roads*. "I lie barefoot and shrimp eyed / in a city that sleeps with a gaping / mouth of ruins."—"Native Stranger".

In "Going", "breathing" is the leitmotif, in the spacing of the words too: Trees, ocean, desert, clouds, various animals, breathe "because there is / nothing / / else to do but breathe". "Carte de Tendre" opens "You don't know what love is, / you sang to me, our legs pretzeled at the end / of the bed, so I did my research and decided / to make myself / a map—" I think Michail does know what love is. Her poems are love poems to people and places. "Gathering Crumbs", for Grandma Estela: "She gathers the crumbs / on the kitchen table, handmade mosaic / a geologist's tender fancy—".

In "Native Stranger":

>   voices intersect   speaking a language I can
>   understand, a language rooted
>   in the land, tightly woven through my
>   spine, a language I can use, a language
>   I can't curse in   a language
>   I don't dream in.

I cannot say exactly where Michail has found her poetry—it is anyway hers and hers alone—but I think it shares with some Greek poets, Elytis comes to mind, a concretized nostalgia, not for the past but for the present–future. Calliope: beautiful-voiced muse of poetry and song. How was it known, in her naming, in the imagining, that Calliope Michail would become that for real? On a pedestal? Yes, I do place *Along Mosaic Roads* on a pedestal, so to speak. Though not one that is fixed. One that is moving, towards roads to come. In "X", "I dance I / dance with paint on my soles."

> Mandelstam in *Stone* quoted by Tsvetaeva in *Earthly Signs*:
> Lord Almighty!—I said by mistake,
> Without thinking to say it at all.

Or my god, my god

Don't make it too much trouble. I am deceived. This so-called Czech beer is brewed in the UK.

I have a most uneasy feeling when a writer I like cites one I do not like. The do not like can be personal or literary or both. If, on the other hand, the writer I like cites one I do like I can nod my head in recognition and appreciation. More often than not this is about contemporaries, contemptible and lovable.

B says
All the leaves
fall off
the trees
A says
I will not argrew
there are still a few
don't be silly
B says

> The fears and the misadventures never leave
> unfinished the imperfect poem of the weave

Quiet. All quiet. "Be quiet." Should the cloth cut in a freedom from vexatious vacancy tenacious tiring an oblique miserable lalalalandscape. What brings you here? Stutter butter. It is a difficult word rather like lalalalanguage. So how do you see and what do you see?

How do your words reveal themselves? They do. But sentences? The least the last other way to rhyme. Embarrassed spelling. In writing. In private. Is it different? To bring into being the beauty of forgetfulness, a temple pressure point. Have you a thing to say? You do. Observe. Tired of dogs dog-eared dog-tired.

Oh disturbance of traffic
I sit like an idiot
askew something is afoot
a kick
a word
that forgets the slightest thing heard

the smells
nuptial uniforms
the bells
it cannot be that you are turned away
this way and that way
in a deeply attractive
explosiveness

In the afternoon of sleep
all here is not right with the world
Is that what you think?
I don't want to hear a bleep
or a kerplunk
out of you

You of the sharp nose and tongue
know your please place
your fate your fête
iniquitous in the world

But I go on nevertheless
not one to stop
or care less
when the champagne cork
goes pop
and there's too much not enough talk

        Infantile rhythms and rhymes
        climate climbs
        I cannot write like the one I like

        Idiot saying
        Why bug me with your cowpat?
        Why why do you do it?

three displaced words I can no longer safely utter
plplplplace lalalalandscape lalalalanguage
they have become dirty words I can only stutter
in my book sucked dry as I would an orange

I begin to fear my shadow even when it is not mine

Idiots poets humans

Where are my sing songs? Everywhere. To hell with the screen a scream.

The many money spider. Do you know what you are doing?

        FINE BOOKS BOUGHT & SOLD
Fine fine. In autumn. Ought & Old. Dropped. You knew

The first wound, whether sacred or secular, all the same . . .
Garlanded. Wreathed. Enrobbed. Ribboned. In name only
Enobled. Enabled. Incapable.

Who are they, those who appear very quickly
Who start startled
Who look for their childhood their children
This day moving so slowly
Unlike some other days
But there is also today a weariness
Apprehend apprehension

—Music.
—What of it?
—Some music is best listened to with the sound turned off. Glass.
 Twinkle twinkle.
—Oh.

Ransacked

NOTHING

How much I might have known was dependent on nothing. But what was nothing? What nothing? I used to think one could not utter just one word and expect it to mean . . . expect its meaning . . . how I like ripping up magazines . . . to shine through in the gloriousness of a single utterance. I think I was wrong. Yet another false start to another central European novel.

> Round the sun
> Round the earth
> Which round
> A pen runs out

You try to hide the lack of sewing with a headband and a tailband. Who are you kidding? Why bother? What are you talking about? Books, my dear, books. Oh, well. That explains nothing.

So, if I were to quote here from an author on god (God) or most likely not-god (-God) it would probably be, easily could be, Imre Kertész. I would want to quote too much so it would be better rather to send the reader straight to his work. *Kaddish for an Unborn Child* for example, or *Kaddish for a Child Not Born* as it was first translated into what is said to be more literal English, in fact in this case more accurate too, since obviously they mean different things, and so A (not I, another A) tells me, newly translated "for no good reason", even if, as K implies, talking about another book, a new translation was, and still is, needed. As bad as each other? Not quite. Anyway I do not care for the way the second translator (in fact the third because the first was a team of two), who became his ubiquitous—a word I do not like—translator, has a penchant, all too frequent, for the awkward redundancy of "as to", in, for example, questions "as to" whether and why (the first translators also do it, though less frequently), as well as, er, other things, such as "in actual fact", of which K tells me there is no trace in the original of *Fateless(ness)*, the other book we have been talking about, to say nothing about the nothing but disservice in the loss of the boy's clumsy voice. (Of course, it is not the boy who has lost his voice, but the translator who has—dumped it for a different kind of clumsiness, the normal kind.) So there, I might say. (If only writers in doubt, if not in doubt they are they should be, read their Fowler. I did and still do. In fact I have to.) So, if I were to quote from another author, Joseph Roth, for example, it would also be better to send the reader straight to his work.

Beautiful names of plants. To get through a difficult time. I have taken days weeks months to change two light bulbs. Couldn't be bothered.

Not to be sure yet every reason to be
esplanades and the dance of a hat
No I do not write down every
windswept word in my hebraic lot

the fury
of the corrugated coruscated
cast-offs and estate sales
because it is in the thinking "what shall I do?"

No, the mulberries are not yet ripe
I travel I unravel away from you
because everything here is soft and held aloft
in the weariness of this world or it is not
gathering some last blackberries
(that's after the mulberries of course and after the dewberries too)
stinging an ankle on some old nettle
shall I write sdrawkcab? no I don't mean that

And you, always you

And how unkind I can learn to be as in I search in vain in the photos of the wiry permed hair frump (her face not her clothes) in her sixties and seventies for a glimpse of the woman I knew in her twenties. I would rather believe it in the elegance of a sister. What madness. Nothing. We are nothing.

And you, not always you

That little upturned nose
That straw hair over the brow
Those hands from the fleece cuffs
But you don't close the door

It is wearing thin. What is? Thin is. Immersed. I was not immersed versed.

The lock is not the same

How is My God to be viewed? Certainly not through a scope. You silly silly boy.

So I have these notes. I cannot for the life of me remember what some of them refer to, or are supposed to mean, for amplification. I mean in *Lamp in the time of the plague* what does *Lamp* mean?

And the rest of you. You all know that but you have kept quiet.

In the mid-1960s, or a little later, I began to write *The Book AM* which began with a line I never got beyond: "I can remember nothing of before I am born." Now, rereading "The Noise of Time" for the umpteenth time I no longer know whether that was mine alone or a reflection of a real life Mandelstam character's "Do I remember what was before my birth? I remember nothing. There was nothing." The letters A and M are the first and middle letters of the alphabet and the initial letters of two given names. I also wrote *Inconceivable Novel* which got listed in *Books in Print* because I sent in the required new publication form. To the occasional library order it was necessary to reply "I'm so sorry your order is inconceivable."

I do what I do not want to do. Like buying another cinnamon bun when one is enough. Tired of being tired. My god. Van Gogh.

Nothing doing. My eye. In Baghdad. That's what one discovers when one goes surfing. Eyeless in Baghdad he assumes under his breath. He admonishes himself. Her too. What an expletive nerve. Explicate?

Yes, another thing to make him nervous. For the sake of his sanity. Don't go any further. Don't watch it. Don't even try to watch it. Don't even read a description. Don't go overboard about this. Nothing about it is explicable. There is a silence.

Do you remember the weeks or months I refused to speak? You are no longer here to remember. When I refused to say anything? Is to say refused to say the right word? Could not? Whatever the right word it was no longer possible. Oh there were reasons. When nothing said is understood or means anything to plural you.

I have tried more than once to write for the theatre. I can't get it to work, except for a couple of squibs. Beckett, Bernhard, of course, would be good models. My most sustained effort attempted to satirize, mostly in a monologue, an ignorant neocolonial literary bureaucrat who ended up a glorified hotel manager in Windsor Great Park. I was sure my piece was lacking. A renewed consensus among a handful of opinions is to dump it. It's dumped.

I think this shows what is possible yet has not been done.

NOVEMBER JOURNAL (2017)

Pascal Quignard is an extraordinary writer who is extraordinarily knowledgeable, about music, myth, history. He is also wrong. His knowledge leads him into wrong. I shall concentrate on one thing. In The Hatred of Music: "It was . . ." Oh, then he is right.

1

What's the point of starting a journal? I've tried it before. What to put in what not to put in. The right word the wrong word. Spontaneous or revised. I would like it to write itself. That idea has always been with me. Want. Would like. Which? Keeping up with momentary thoughts.

Yesterday I wrote asking V if he has an opinion about Quignard. After all, they are both philosphers. He doesn't answer that. Only comments on, confirming, in other words, my extraordinary and confusing.

No word from Y about Rotterdam.

Sh is still sleeping. She would like to go to Brighton, an awful place, today, to the good fish restaurant where you sit on a stool at a counter-like table. But the sun is half out. Sh hates the sun. The sun you love, she says. Autumn the only season that suits England. Sh is awake.

I have lost a document on the laptop. It must be there somewhere. Perhaps I must go to Time Machine. Yes. newwritingnotes restored. Somehow I must have deleted it by mistake. Time Machine works. This one does.

I am sneezing like mad today. Allergy. Dust?

You see, a short walk for a prescription (not the allergy), an idea occurs to me, speak to the receptionist, walking back, it's gone, whatever I had to say it's gone. If it was of any use it will come again. Oh, I have remembered: They do not answer. They have no intention of answering.

I am catching up on many unread books by Max Frisch and Pascal Quignard. And Bernhard's *Collected Poems* has just arrived. That last translated so-so. Many, not all, published by Seagull, who publish quite a few good books and quite a few bad ones and quite a lot of deadwood by otherwise good authors. To be expected. But the publisher does not answer a letter, or these days an email. He is a frequent recipient of grants.

I wrote a not very good play about a director of the Africa Centre, then literature (huh) director of the British Council, then the Arts Council, then a glorified hotel manager in Windsor Great Park. It's no secret who he is. I can't do it. It's no good. It shouldn't be published. Anyway, it will do you no good, as it is said. Employed by the intelligence (huh) services no doubt at all. [But now it is.]

Lovely lunch at Riddle & Finns. Sole for Sh. Boulliabaise. But I tell them the Schweppes must go. Poison does not go with poisson.

2

I don't have to write every day.

I would like to have engaged with SP over her pointless article in G but it's probably not possible. On another matter I am reminded too that had she read my book on HC first, or paid attention to what she must have read in his own book, which she did read, she would not have been party to that stupid error in the BBC talk about NC.

3

Reading in twilight on a bench near the ruins while Sh is riding her compact bike. Fell off just as I was getting on.

Haven't moved my car all week for fear of losing a parking place on the 5th. Except this year it is the 4th, a Saturday. My one end street is the only one in the vicinity where cars can stay.

4

Just this minute a lovely email from Kl in Paris. She is lovely. Such a surprise. I should think better of myself.

And to think that I was just about to moan about how I am living in the wrong town. I don't like opera. I don't like bonfire. I don't need to think such thoughts when a message such as hers arrives.

Tomorrow is the premiere of *Unfinished Concerto*.

5

A great deal of effort not to feel miserable almost all day. Loggerheads. Anxious. Nervous. Irritated. Subdued. Nothing new of course. Any reason at the moment might be an excuse. Where to position a word. The size of the house. Forehead burning up.

6

Oh my God, Oh my goodness, For God's sake. Which God are we invoking?

Sh is laughing this morning. Hates the sun which is out in the cold today. Says C and other of my friends must think she is my imaginary friend, like a child has.

The Salon at Wütternberg. Written 1980s. Set in 1960s. At least this part: the narrator takes a woman "to lunch at a farm restaurant [the translation] at Ouville-l'Abbaye". But it's a small place. Little there. X says there was once a pub by the Marie. But that doesn't sound like it.

So many stupid intelligent people. I don't exclude myself.

7

More flirtatious texts with R.

A message from Y during the night. I should not look at my iphone during the night. Things still not clear enough. I had to deal with it during the night before I could go back to sleep. Regretfully I have said no to his Rotterdam festival.

Sh to Paris today for a few days. Paris Photo expo.

8

Notes from the iPhone from the last two or three weeks:

You are neither a comedy nor a tragedy unless you are a laughing stock

If this is who they are

I once stood on the jetty where the scream and the girls stood. It isn't a bridge, often so called. A jetty

It is never over. Is that the tragedy?

There is a reason why the queen can do anything she wants. While the king is hemmed in. One false move

Unbearable music without space

These are notes to myself. No need for anything other than initials

Thyme tea. Tinnitus

As if history could not be settled

iPhone crashed during update last night. Incomprehensible at least to a layman error messages. Fortunately restored this morning with no loss of data e.g. these notes. What would we do what did we do before?

Winter tyre wheel change this morning. Last year turned out pointless. Will there be good snow this year?

Why should one not take one's empties back to the bar on leaving? Less incentive for the tables to be wiped clean.

This little house has no fireplace. I gaze at a nightlight candle.

Shall I incorporate my few "newwritingnotes"? What should go where? What should go in *The Making of a Story* and what should not?

9

Oh it's tiresome. So many translators and/or their editors are incapable of understanding that in English bilberries are not (wild) blueberries—whatever they are called in other languages—and that whiskey and whisky are different drinks. There are scant few blueberries, a mainly American native, in the wild in Europe, except for such as escapes. There are a multitude of bilberries which should not be translated as (wild) blueberries. It is wrong to translate into whiskey what is obviously whisky in the original. Or less frequently vice versa. True there are occasions when the intended spirit is not clear, but not often. (And there is even one USA bourbon, Maker's Mark, which is whisky!) [Rick Stein wrongly says blueberries in Iceland. Alan Garner rightly says bilberries in *Where Shall We Run To?*]

It is one thing to smile. It is another to be smug even if embarrassed. Loathsome, both, P and B have plans. Obviously. From bad to worse.

I hope Brexit is an utter failure, in whatever form that failure takes. I don't have to hope. It is. 'Tis what we deuxœufs—unœuf.

10

What a good idea! Y suggests we skype during his festival.

11

If only someone with the authority, Dismayhem, or whoever, had the courage to stand up and say, No, this will not work, there will be no Brexit.

12

I don't know what to read.

13

R

14

Sh has brought calissons back from her trip to Paris. Multicoloured. Not the plain original ones.

15

Paragraphs on S and C for L's third transcriptions compilation. Very pleased to have been asked.

17

Last night's *Snow* event at Magazine warm and friendly. Good supper at Mange Tout opposite afterwards, though the duck and the sea trout took rather long to arrive. Breakfast with I and K at their hotel this morning before they left for home. R couldn't make it. Parental duties. C read R's work. CM down from London. Sh took photos.

18

Y's festival today. No skype for their technical reasons. N showed his films at Depot in the afternoon. Good discussion. No problems with the projector.

23

I have missed too many days. Things to write about. Ginette's passing on Sunday so to Paris today until Monday. The service is tomorrow.

29

Sweet meeting for tea with Kl at Ladurée rue Bonaparte last Saturday.

An architect so I presented her with N's *Unbuilt Netherlands* and all *Snow*. Photo. Visited X family in their new apartment Sunday. Twenty thousand steps to and fro across Paris. Not much desire to write at the moment. Not true. I want to but do not want to.

*

"Gentleman."

I have Tanizaki's *The Maids* open. She of the slender nimble foot on tiptoe to reach across the counter till.

And you, you are the most unflustered. You have the appearance of one who is most comfortable with herself.

IT IS THE MOUNTAIN

It is the mountain. *Á* mountain. The accent-ascent is not the best. Thee mountain. All mountains. The sum-summit of the mountains. From one window the pale grey wall of a house looks like a mountain, if I close my eyes, the shutters. But the wall is brick not stone.

Why?—discourteous question, whatever it is about, life, loves . . . while I fiddle with a glyph, thinking I must have nothing better to do. *Why not* is a different matter when it is an affirmation. Just as a diacritic is very interesting. Mystical.

Senseless.

*

The heart it gave out too many days

Damn you god

B
"might raise an
eyebrow and tap her foot"
tra la la

It is the loveliest thing

Your god is a jealous god
And nothing is enough.
D'you mean everything?
No, nothing.

Indeed I have drawn you to the dawn

It's fine
to be a Valentine
who you are my dear
I've an idea

O to answer a statement with a yes or a no it is the same
and must be understood it is not a question

What is the point

diesen Singsang voll Unverstand

Mariupol
You are remembered always
Your children, humanity
Your theatre, of war
We remember
You remember
        Bucha and   22 March–April 2022

Do you know the wonderful song
The moment I wake up
Before I put on my make-up
I say a little prayer for you
Of course I don't wear make-up
The moment I wake up
I think of you

read
Ingeborg Bachmann's *Three Paths to the Lake*
on war photography

My little intelligence agent says
Little me in my flowery smocks
Tease the boys in my little white lies, I, I mean, socks

Oh find me an old ramshackle
house with a big garden
scrump words

a dozen chocs he ate
'cause he hates
it when he doesn't

Sing along sing along

Her legs are crossed
cross

Forehead eruptions are
blemishes from the past

Drink from the stone

So many dusts
motes
dawn
I may stare not even unto space
thinking   little time to spare for the practical

but for the bacon of the wild boar
I would not want to be
on the wrong side of Bea
with her baton or oar

a blemish
on stupid music

Let us pray in rubbles

It is not funny
though it is a comic book prize
because of the money
through the cosmic shock
lies

our lives
not lie

To grasp the full horror hurrah
comic book nothing
funny about this.

They do the same.
Who is They?
It says They

in the comic book.
You wrote it.
I did.

You touch theatre

Not if I can help it

There is no word
Isn't there

Fragments of my love

What if I did buy a book I already had. Either I couldn't find it or I couldn't be sure. Indelicate balance. I don't understand the books I read, I said. But I do know when to write wine bottles and when to drink a bottle of wine, I said, to my, if not anyone else's, amusement. O good old bosom bread. And an ancient recipe.

I came out of my dream. I thought: this is an hallucinatory story. I'm inside one of my poems. Half-alluding to a story by Tabucchi. The aeroplane is on the ground. It is red. This illusionary key might be the key to misunderstanding.

I was in the middle of reading a book by Antonio Tabucchi, yes, really, about halfway through, when the postman delivered a book by Yoko Tawada, which I turned to. . . . And now I've forgotten. Things in both books or in one of them are confused. And now I don't remember. Except stone. Stone is definitely in both.

But my heart wasn't in it. It's always the heart. This irritation of the shoulder blade. Precocious flowering of the skirt—

Who can say if I alone am inventing?

That's right walk off camera.

I saw a magpie hopping between the flowers, respectfully

—So where are the sing songs then?
—Embedded.

Phrasing and phasing of the moon. Fading fasting.

Acts of imputiny

The miracle of the world and the living

You want to destroy

Indelible incredible inedible

Decisions decisions and my lack of certain knowledges
dispersed wait lies
the morning of a chocolate mourning
the scribble of a tousled hair
knowing and not knowing
the cathedral and the dog
the look in the dog's eyes
the unusual step on the ping-stones
nowhere else is this done
and what a mop up

At the dinner I asked, Why are you never in the audience? Arrogan said, I am a producer of culture, not a consumer. Throw 'im out.

Rebec, who is not a musical instrument, although she is musical, says,

There are days and days that go by where I almost forget about writing, and then I see my small pile of notes and printed scripts and it's a little odd, like I'm not sure who they belong to. How beautiful is what she says.

Is there a history of bookmarks? I don't know. I'll look. Yes, there seems to be.

I DO NOT THINK ELSE LASKER-SCHÜLLER IS HOLDING A FLUTE IN HER FAMOUS PHOTO

I think it is an instrument with single reeds, described technically as a clarinet. It could be a Sardinian three-pipe launeddas, with the third pipe, which you cannot see, also to her lips. More probable it is a double pipe of north Africa, Arabia, or Turkey, which goes by many names, one of which is mizmār.

Why I am allowed to be here I do not know. I come for some comfort. The ligature might well work for a script but not more, or work loose. Weary, is that a better word? The one sticks out. The one does not. Movement. Moment. Be my daughter my sister my love—
What is your role, when you are not serving rolls?
There is rather too much noise today, squealing.
You are very efficient. Industrious.
I want to start squealing too. No, not really.
Today you are my comfort. You, of whom I know next to nothing.
But I write about you.
Ponytail.
On other days, a bun. Oh, a bun.
No wonder. Cuchicuchicoo.
Keep open your eyes.

What do you see? What do you say?

Questions are certainly questions, are they not? I delete you but I cannot. I sit down at the table, to write a little. I refuse to be classed. I would love us to be clasped.

Mosaic. Your programmed pogrom. Morphed. You run into your ruin. You betray your portrait. Ear. Compete complete complication. Oh how I sit in the cold. Something, anything, to latch on to to explain ... Why look forward? Why urge? Why pour out your heart? Almighty heart. Fascination. Assassination. Your god is a jealous god. Time whiles away. There are still songs to sing.

Both are honoured with wine paraphernalia and school book prizes.

For whom does one write? For the one who one day will say, oh, my goodness, how wonderful, how beautiful, how true (true?), how is it that just a few were able to acknowledge that they knew and understood (knew and understood?) what the writer wanted to write.

> Thank you Greta for
> My clover
> Its leaves are over
> Three for they are four

Anxiety. Nameless an x y a z

Brought up face to face little ones with huggy dolls each night I might mouth a line from my translation or my child's poem aleviate anxiety for a wish

Without a book I may or may not be able to write

God given. Do not forsake my darling on this our bedded day. God forgiven God forbid. He decided to cry, not to cry.

CLARICE LISPECTOR

I wrote an essay about Clarice Lispector, "A Disaccumulation of Knowledge", collected in my book of critical essays *Antonyms Anew: Barbs & Loves* (2016). I said in anticipation: "*Discovering the World*, Lispector's near complete [it doesn't claim completeness] *Crônicas*, translated by Giovanni Pontiero, was published by Carcanet in 1992. It is long out of print but about two thirds were reissued in 1996 by New Directions as *Selected Crônicas*. This is still in print though it would not surprise if a new translation is in the offing." And so it was.

I considered writing a full review but I may be out of my depth. This will have to suffice. It is a complaint about style, not about accuracy (though an obvious lack of intelligibility does sometimes stare you in the face). In 2022 New Directions in USA and Penguin Classics in UK published a new translation, by Margaret Jull Costa and Robin Patterson, under the miserable, tiresome, title *Too Much of Life: Complete Chronicles* (which it really is not because some of these newspaper pieces appear to be missing, and not only those whose omission is half-heartedly justified along the way in a footnote, although there are entries from other, pre-1967 and post-1973, sources, and an interesting afterword by one of Lispector's sons). Why this new translation? Pontiero's original, clearly a labour of love, is beautiful, with absolutely appropriate cadences. It doesn't jar. The new translation often does. Too often one is, or I am, brought up short by a thoughtless, pedestrian, stumbling block. It is, in this respect, not that well written. No accounting for the unusualness of Lispector's Portuguese makes that good. Read any entry and then go back, if you can, to Pontiero's translation and I think you will see that the Costa–Patterson—there is no indication of individual or collaborative roles—is not as right as you might first have expected.

There is a vacancy

Your dog is a noise polluter barking it's head off in the town's pedestrian precinct, can hardly call it a square, I wanted to tell the owner, whose fault it was, not the dog's but I did not not wanting to add to the disturbance. Anyway, what was I doing loitering on a bench reading a book by, ha, Robert Walser

I fell over reaching up to pick a pear half-hidden among the leaves. Be careful.

Excuse me but dogs are not allowed in here. There are cast-iron notices at the entrances. Nor is cycling permitted nor ball games. Anyway what am I doing loitering on a bench rereading a book by, yes, Robert Walser

Excuse me. Dogs are not allowed in here —I'm autistic and I am allowed. Her little dog on a lead

Excuse me. Dogs are not allowed in here —I didn't know —There are notices at the entrances —I'm blind. He is wearing dark glasses. It is not a guide dog he has on a lead. He does not have a white stick. A woman accompanies him who is not blind

I think I had better keep quiet

Heart sinks at the mention. But not the heart

Too hot or too cold

Sometimes it is enough

CONVERSATION WITH MY GOD

Did you make dinosaurs? Of course not. You didn't make them up? Who could ever summon such! If not you? They are the vivid imagination of people's fears. Did you make people? Fears? You'll have to ask them, quite a few think so. Deluded? It's only a joke. A "crude joke"? There's a question. And your son?
My son. My daughter. My

[Rereading Qian Zhongshu's *Limited Views* I find there is little about you, God, that I can add to what he says. For example, the section entitled "The Demonic and the Divine includes the essays "Ghosts and Gods", "More Joy on Earth than in Heaven", "Time in Heaven, Earth, and Hell", "Rebuking Heaven", "Poets in Hell".]

Frightened for life
An imperial tragedy treasury
In reference in reverence
A logical princess with a dispassionate ring in her ear
Oh sun whereforartthou oh sun
There is a stampede
There is a draft in the air
From whizzing missiles

Yes, there is a draft in the air and I am unable to write intelligibly about one of my ancestral homelands . . .

. . . I begin to reread a book picked from a pile, one I must have read already though nothing I am reading reminds me that I have until I come across an annotation in the margin in my writing with an "ugh" against the clumsy way the translator has handled a particular sentence . . .

Here is an empty

It was but isn't
It isn't lace
It isn't pheasant

REB REBEC REBECCA

Reb is a traditional Jewish form of address, corresponding to Sir. Rebec, derived from Arabic rabāb, is a medieval stringed instrument. Rebecca appears in the Hebrew Bible. She is Rebecca. So Rebecca is Rebecca. This Rebecca is Rebecca. Reb A plays his rebec for Rebecca. Reb A would serenade Rebecca if he could but he doesn't get on well with stringed instruments with more than one string. Rebecs usually have three. A is more at home as a percussionist and bamboo flautist, and with other things. A has several one-string instruments, from Asia. He also has a stringed instrument with no strings. A cheeseboard in the shape of a violin, perhaps, because of its size, a viola. Without a wire to cut the cheese.

SPEECHLESS

—More often than not the Nobelit leaves me, what shall I say, speechless. Award winning author. Award winning this and that. A new lit prize. The Snowball Prize. —Is that an actual prize? —No! Don't be silly. —It ought to be. —Nobel snobel sleighbells snowball or fall. —It wouldn't be worth much. —When it falls on you it fulminates in a puff of powder. —There's a children's story there. —Mr Snowfall and the Piece Prize.

You are evading the serious nature of the things you really want to write about with your little amusements. The procatinator is at work. Pouring with the right hand a steaming cup from a coffee kettle, left elbow on the table, fist supporting the cheek. No wafting cigarette smoke though. You are flaunting your failings. Your belles-lettres.

So, Мистер Кремль. What have you done? Мистер Крамбль. Confiscated fruit. It is a given.

"But it *is* a mistake. A mistake carved on stone, right here in front of us."

Do not lean back on the put-you-up, with or without a book, immediately after you have eaten, especially things like nuts, almonds, say. You may splutter and choke. You must sit up quickly and recover.

What you covert you may not convert for the poem has no home except in itself. Reb awakes. The uniformed is uninformed. There is a smell of burning and there is smoke. It is hair. Temptation is of the berry and to cap it all many go cup in hand. Colour is obviously a distraction because it interrupts the interpreter. It is a mishmash.

"I don't wear perfume"

The unicorn of course on the other hand exists. God made me forget my homework. God works. Out like a light. God has uses.

Pascal Quignard really should read Mori Ōgai, if he has not already done so. Probably he has. Q's koi philosophy.

SCHOOL POEM
Bea returns to school tomorrow
How I hope it's not with sorrow
A magpie's chatter may wake her up
She'll drink her milk up in a cup
She'll skip her way up the street, or is it down
The way to town

4 Sept 22

TYPO

To ameliorate his longing across the table he wrote her a note. Which at least on reflection might give her a frisson of excitement even if fright as well. After all, he was writing, trying to, a story as she also might be. But were his nerves shaking because he had walked across the light and airy café to place the note on her table, "This is for you", or because of the four-shot espresso, quadruple he liked to call it on the exceptional occasions on which he ordered it, he had just finished. This is more or less the note he gave her written on a paper napkin because although he had a pen in his coat pocket he had no paper. A fine thing for a so-called writer:

Well it is true that you do look rather lovely

He had the feeling he was continuing in reality what he was reading in the novel he was reading

He thought it more likely that rather than reply to him she might wait till they came across each other again.

She had not replied yet. If she reappeared the next Wednesday, for it was only on two Wednesday's he had come across her in the café, he could assume that she was not averse to his approach, or that she did not really care one way or the other. If, on the other hand, she did not appear, baring any other reason he could not know about, it would be because she was averse and wanted to avoid him. Then he would feel guilty for having driven her away from her working place. He was writing part of this in the café.

She did remind him of Ah, who said she loved him (he thought she had) and whom he loved, though, for example, the colour of her hair was quite different, being black not auburn-like. They had both worn blue dungarees. Ah in a photo she sent him. She on the first time he saw her. Looking at her inspired him

As if he did not have the confidence to believe that she really did love him

I did not at first think I recognized Iz when she entered the café and stood looking toward me from the counter. She was different, well, not terribly, but enough, with a touch of the gothic, well, not really, made up, and hair differently from before. Plonked herself down at a table I think was her favourite, actually slap bang in front of but not looking at me, typing intensely, intently later relaxing her left elbow reassured

Arriving home he is astonished to receive a text nessage: "Hi, this is Iz. I am a writer in fact! Maybe I'll see you in the cafe another time."

Thighs

"I'm afraid I cannot meet today. Sorry." "Thank you for letting me know" and said she might send me some piece of her writing to read, if she wished.

Do not go this Wednesday. If you do and she is not there you will be both relieved and disappointed. If she is there and you are not, she may wonder.

Now she has a plait and large black-rimmed glasses. Black dungaree dress. Coffee in a glass, croissant. Once again, for the third time at least, she is different but the same. Furious upright concentrated typing. As if she does not know I am writing about her and was in this café before her doing just that. Of course not. But talk? It does not seem possible. Not yet, anyway. I suppose I could send her a text across the tables. Not a good idea. Just carry on working. Oh, silly, I have sent her a text: "Wish I could type as well as you do. Only two fingers for me." She will not get it yet. The text message is green not blue delivered. Oh well, it is funny. It might be ice breaking. Not fraught. Heavens, she is looking at her phone. Back to typing. Back to phone. Back to typing. OK, home. This again at a time of mostly silence from Ah. —Ah, a little message from Ah.

(Some of what follows and some of what came before is out of sequential chronology. I think that must be tautologous.)

Saturday morning, 25 March. I am rereading Qian Zhongshu, *Humans, Beasts, and Ghosts*. It is months since that first note. Is that her? Her hair is different again. Beautiful dress to her ankles. I'm just not sure. A little later, she presents herself at my table. Now I am sure. Now I am delighted and at first not a little lost for words. She introduces herself. I invite her to sit opposite. We chat. She writes short prose and poetry. She studies literature and philosophy. We shake hands. She goes back to her work. In her own good time.

Oh, it is a dance. Recreant or sagacious. Here the Metamir would be useful. Or is it the rain? I was not up to it though I was when I woke up

The book lies on the bed cover and I am under it on my side.

"Of course those eminences did not believe in faerie fotos. They must have been having us on."

The river comes before or after

Life relief
Rusted earth

There was Once upon a time or as I once said Once upon a spacetime continuum there was

Crestfallen fallen cherry leaf

Still there are things to be found. There is much I do not know.

White sheets and blackouts

Fascination

The tyrant reasons why should you live in peace. And why should I. Why should one live or why should one not. Non peace mirroring peace. There you are: a refrain from the coy homophone.

G<small>D</small>, to be sure.

A few books, piled precariously, have tumbled off the shelf. Let them lie where they are for the moment.

This book is a bit of a mess, no matter.

Careful, the holly book stings.

In *Too Loud a Solitude* Bohumil Hrabal, under the guise of his alter ego Haňťa: "If I knew how to write, I'd write a book about the greatest of man's joys and sorrows."

I cast an eye over the fitness exerciser and think I am fit.

14 FEBRUARY 2023
This heart you can break because it's made of chocolate

*

It may be a bird of prayer

Light be
Light was

My God, pernicious utterance attraction

Let us persist

Very determined fast typist

But then I begin to wonder. Is this the same person.

Streaks across the sky

Not the one I thought she was in the glare of her skirt

Obscenity of the cross

How on earth, and in heaven, did they believe this stuff

She is looking at me. Studying

Not to be earthbound but to balance on a branch

And the covers warm you.

How could I doubt you

He lay the book down beside him on the duvet not on the side table. So that it accompanied him or he it he thought

It had always happened. Had always been like that

Again I was not sure I recognized her until I looked at—

Here by some default or fault

You walk as if you are setting out on a journey. Determined stride even in a smallish room. And you walk with a bounce across the same room

"I'm so sorry your order has only just gone through to the kitchen in case you are wondering why your food is taking so long. "That's all right" looking up from a book.

There she is again. Different again. Very girly. Hair streaked with blue like last time.

"Good morning Iz." Hand wave.

"I'm very busy."

Past altered by present future

I clap my hand around an annoying fruit fly but I don't really want to kill it. It's harmless. Unlike when I clap my hand around a clothes or flour moth.

Sadness and sorrow

FURTHER NOTE ON THE INFINITE

In an essay "Saddened by a Height" Qian Zhongshou invokes, among others, Ungaretti's poem "Stasera" beginning "Balaustrata di brezza", Leopardi's *Zibaldone* (and in a different essay "L'Infinito"), Alice in *Through the Looking Glass*, and eleventh-century Su Shi who has a poem in which he counsels not to use the finite to pursue the infinite.

I think I can see where to go

"Ah, science, you killer of dreams."—Hettie Judah, *Lapidarium: The Secret Lives of Stones*, Murray, 2022

Leopardism

"London first."
"You know I hate London."

Do not approach her.

Oh, there she is sitting on my favourite bench under the fig tree, where she has seen me before, waiting for her beau or her friend. "Hallo." "Hi."

Frisson not fright

Appraise the twig for the world does tend to tell its own story, which says little about the word, if you will forgive the familiar, my dear Calvino, and, as I think you seem to say, the story has no end because (when, if) it has no beginning.

"I love my new ring" heard said. There was a sweet smell of rot. Who named and there she is again different again. Daffodilism. He stared at the dust he cannot bring himself to dust. Comforting smock desultory. Quiet desperation. Deep seated dejection

To call a halt. If you, dear possible reader, find the writing disjointed disappointed I cannot say no it is not. To pick up some at least of the pieces as best as possible.

Admired and admitted. An eternity of destiny. So upright in her neat beauty. Possibly positively sporty. A navel novel. A notion nation. What is it I see in her mouth? There she is, standing. Almost a military bearing soldier. There for the god of love most certainly not for the love of god. Scatter my ashes under the mulberry tree one day? Bury me under the history of stone? Sediment sentiment. Determined stride. Those things again. A declination. Subsiding subsisting subsidizing a catalytic cataclysmic cataclysm.

The reader. Holding the book dozing.

Intuition tuition

History is unfinished.

Women have eyes in the backs of their heads. Or is it the sides? Whatever, usually they know when they are being looked at

In one version of the myth in the dream she is seen grinning while she reads his message

Demure

I did dream. You wrote a poem. One of those spaced out across the page ones. Among other things I do not remember you said leave false hopes and enjoy small things in life. I try both with varying degrees of success. Do you know how long ago it is that you first and afterwards often said how much you missed me?

O golly
How shoddy
The foot of the poem

Heavy paving slab step has shifted in the Gar*den*

It's time to stop this nonsense

Nel went to France
In her summer frock
She wore a wide-brimmed hat
And on a seat she sat
Or on a rock
And I daresay she ate an orange too

> Look at those eyes
> Look at those sighs

AUGUST

There is a harmless, presumably, madman in this town—not our idiosyncratic (I choose the word with deliberation) hereditary lord who might one day make it into a different story . . . I see him in our Gardens. He wears crazy clothes. A mop of straw hair splays out from beneath a winter beanie. Is he a scarecrow? He airs his laundry, which he wheels around, along with other belongings, in a supermarket trolley, on the protective railings surrounding the mulberry. Yesterday evening he was wheeling his trolley, not that it is his, on the red brick path past the bench on which I was sitting under the ripened quince. He edged close and paused to ask in a mumble what I was reading. With some winsome exceptions I do not like that at the best of times, though I am not averse to doing it myself if the occasion suggests itself, but usually I reply obligingly politely. But I slammed the book shut saying it was my business, using that hateful word. He chuckled and moved on. Instinctively, I had a reason for doing this of which I was not fully aware until some seconds later. I was, as I thought, reading Strindberg's *A Madman's Defence*. Not a good idea to show that to a madman. But I had finished rereading that book a few days ago. The book I was reading now was *Inferno* and *From An Occult Diary*, in one volume, showing Edvard Munch's lithograph of the author's head on the cover. —Oh, my goodness, yesterday was Sunday, 27th August. August Strindberg. So today is August bank holiday Moonday.

I raise two fingers to your governmental clichés british public tax payer money value fair values never happen again get to the bottom compensate late insufficient innocence dead blood post wrongful rush tests clad forgotten zero tolerance inquiry transparent promise to be honest no I am not enigmatic

Seen
Hell
Nothing new
Rupture rapture
Daggers down drawn
My word. Myth of

My head thrown back
My elbows stretched out not held tight to the side
My shephardic flute

Idiodic

> A dusty mess
> I wish it were less

Is it you? Exciting?

—Finished. —What is finished? —Use your imagination. —I have no imagination. Only . . . —What? —Ellipsis

mid October 2023

The badness of Headlong

As I lean forward to put the book on the low table the cushion behind my head flops and gives me a gentle shove in the back as if to say, do do something, do get up

HERE LIES A

MONUMENTAL LIAR

Who is the or|the of this book?

How intriguing your slenderness, towering, a lankiness not at all ungraceful contrary to the dictionary definitions, and your at first seemingly sour mouth, which is not sour at all when you speak and burst into laughter. I open the door and there you are disembarking from a footstool. —I didn't think you had grown that tall today. —Ha, no. Then you say, My dear, with my coffee. My heart goes out to you. It is so delightful to look into your face, which is not much wider than your neck. You are eating your lunch on a street bench. I'd like us to talk. A rag doll. A peg doll. Straw. No and Yes. It's as if you had stepped out of the pages of a fairy tale, long ago.

To pay for one's mistakes?
To elevate the word in its use.

STORY BEFORE CHRISTMAS

"I'd like to get the *Ravilious* book from you for Xmas. If you give me lokum only my stomach knows it for a short while. But the book I can know it forever."

And I have lost my bookmark, my place, like a dream.

HERE LIE THE RUINS OF
FOUR REDACTED PARAGRAPHS

       Close your eyes and visualize
       The image magic

       A glimpse
       More than a glimpse

                *

Iz is Ir. Caution and curiosity

Silk shift

            MY THOUGHTS
     Should I bury my head in the sand
      or whatever else is to hand?

     gazing into a pond is to ponder
           she adds:
     "Lakely I have been pondering"
       a second she adds:
        "I'm all dried up"

      In which sense do I suspire?
        no oreads but naiads

He wondered whether her giving him the two naiad pictures, so lovely, and on the Feast of Saint Valentine, showed that she trusted him, not to fall, or that she wanted him to fall, into the pond. Because even though he was, he believed, free now, he believed he knew that she was not. If he fell would she offer him her slender hand, or murmur, the slough of despond, it is where you belong? Anyway, there was age to think about. Innocence.

While I was writing that passage I felt as if I were adding a passage to Italo Svevo's *Zeno's Conscience*, which I happened to be rereading at the time, or to another of his works with not dissimilar scenes, as I still do. I more or less offered that as one of two feeble excuses. If I had not been immersed in Zeno's conscience I might not have written that passage, which, anyway, I had not expected would create such turmoil and vehement protestation—one sentence is a later addition. At most a rap on the knuckles if it did not amuse her, as I had expected it would but which it did not. Yet had I been so wrong to reveal a not unimaginable effect those pictures, of which one at least was quite alluring, in their way, might produce? Oh, Stop! What was the point of all this if it was no more than a fiction, and Svevo had already written it, and said everything that could be said? Apart from Beckett, of course, for one. No. I was not wrong. Not so wrong.

Have some things taken their toll? They certainly add up. Would I receive a sensible message? I'm not holding my breath, not any longer. I have decided, against her ipse dixit wishes, that I shall not have removed her work from the review when it is published later in the year. With her copies, I shall include a note to the effect that I am not prepared to see her hurt more than she is already over what amounts to no more than misreadings—on one of or both our parts. I have thought carefully how to word this. Eggshells. Eggshells.

It is February and it is a leap year. I was right not to hold my breath. I decided after all I should tell her why I would not remove her work. Weeks later she replied asserting her copyright to remove her work. Done. It is October. There has been an exchange, a change. All seems well.

"I saw her words had created a new world, like all words that are not true."—Zeno

O mOst perfect rOundness nOw the eye settles

Is it tomorrow yet?

"Because I haven't told everything."—God the God and other things, forgiveness, for example. Look again at Lispector, Lagerkvist.

Reputation repudiation

But she has a lost look. Does have. Short strides as if about to embark on journeys

"I woke up after noon and saw that the moon needed painting."

You have lost your History. For bad. Forbad. Historicity

Damned publishers. Always up to something, or nothing

So (you) return to your designs your fabrications

Harness harass

Perception is, almost, everything

The seamy side of the fabric.

Lead sheets. Lead roofs

Invalidated invalid

I would like to be able to snowboard

More than a glimpse
Staying straying

atone stone

conversion conversation

What shall I do with these misread or misheard words?

Insight inside

Do you think you can plonk any old word onto the paper, and that it will be meaningful? That you can get away without excercising yourself more? —Yes, sometimes. Like Lispector wanting to write without having to write.

It is my will

> POEM FOR NELLY
> Nelly loves her locks
> They're made of cauliflower
> She also loves her smocks
> With many a coloured flower

I was reading Saramago's *The Stone Raft*, in which the Iberian Peninsular breaks away from Europe, and sails out to sea. It opens with a personage throwing a heavy stone an impossible superhuman distance. The next book I open is Gombrowicz's *Polish Memories* where I read the phrase "a stone's throw". What these two rereadings have to do with each other I do not know, except for their proximity.

am aim intaminated

WHAT IS WRONG WITH THIS TOWN

Not forgetting that there are some things that are not wrong. And that things are probably not much different in any other town. How stocked with poets we are. Your Majesties! Artists even more so. A mournful trumpet busker practising in the precinct to music minus one. I'd like to say put some life into it but I'm sure he can't. It doesn't matter what he's playing, "As Time Goes By", "Dancing Cheek to Cheek", it's all the same. I can't find walzerian or Walserian joy in any of this (oh, but there is a good trombone player). Dogs in cafés, yapping, yelping, or not. Artisan double espressos, so often so sour (not bitter, sour). Not-so-convenience seats shifting under the butt (that's the backslide). Shall I go on with other things that ought to be disposed of, and will be when I'm elected president of the republic (off wiv 'iz 'ead, that's right 'ead not read)? Instant caff (insult to the bean), white chocolate (it's not chocolate), neckties (phallic flagging), single-sex schools (unless . . . oh, no, I've been advised not to crack that jocularity), cricket (hours wasted in the outfield waiting for a ball that never arrives and missing it when it does), mayonnaise, crème fraîche (whitey-yellowy paint poured, spooned, over unsuspecting dishes that might otherwise be edible, or delectable—mustard ok custard not ok). There's more but that's enough. I'd need to be a Gombrowicz to bring off accusations, or a Hrabal if I wanted to be more amused. Somewhere, ages ago, I wrote of Hrabal's *The Little Town Where Time Stood Still* . . . Not exactly my (I, I mean this) town of twittens and twits, our (its) version of narrow streets and narrow minds in other towns others have written off (I, I mean of). But close enough. Breweries. And here's another thing, however unrelated: Fibre. Fibre is the route to the laptop and the lap.

Ah, a very silly child or a not very nice grown-up. Or a bit of both?

IN THE LAND OF IKAN
Duologue between interrogator and terror suspect

What is your name?

Notonyourlifewho.

What! You won't tell me your name?

I just did.

Oh, I see. Are you charged?

I am chargé d'affaires.

Are you attached?

I am attaché. I am attached to my land.

This land is my land.

Mine.

Mine.

Mine.

Mine. How confusing.

God said it was mine.

Said? Was? What if God was wrong? What if there is no God?

Was? Is? Then I say it is mine. Our weapons are better than yours.

So you say. For the moment.

What else can I do?

Goodness knows. Ikannot.

14 April 2024

Untruths

A Swiss miss in France

I often wonder if lost contacts might see themselves in the books

A touch of the gothic. Quite changed

Expulsion of the apologia

Who in hell wants peace?

matsu is both pine and wait in Japanese, a little like English, I pine for you, but only when you say it because the Japanese are homophones and the letters are different and there are other matsu, such as edge, splash, an abbreviation for jasmine

Cosmic cosmo

Residue of race

At cross purposes

Whose twilight of the

Effort affect

Unearing

The lambs the iambs

I am sitting in a bookshop one of a chain

I know I have next to nothing to do with or it me

A confused confess
Troth truth

How quick the crying
The laughter

borrow burrow

I doubt that I have anything new or useful to say but I'll say it anyway

Old loves, if that's what they were, good and bad, won't leave me alone. Lusts

(Still born)

Have I been it feels like it put out to grass in the green parts of this town and other places such as the numerous cafés where once there were very few

If we had a Stalinist regime which writers? Who would denounce? Who would just be quiet?

The way you move to the music. Golden princess. Capture a glimpse

No experiment. Just achievement. Or not

Wo bist du?

Back the paving

His ears rang

His early song

And who will put out the light
When he wants to read

Indignant indigent

"Remember Russia in general, which still exists somewhere and may return to you someday but never to me." —Nina Berberova, *The Book of Happiness*, trans. Marian Schwartz

abysmal baptismal

Petals of the lily how "I would love to" pinkish

I think of an affinity between Clarice Lispector and Elsa Morante. For example, in Lispector's last book I imagine Morante writing parts of Angela's dialogues with Author, the man who has given Angela *A Breath of Life*. It is Angela, not Author, who speaks for Lispector.

With a little skip

Symbolic soul

Broken down in small pieces

Nothing nothing is too much trouble

O, the present must be an abstraction because it flows from the future to the past without a plausible pause

The cross crosses me. The star and the crescent are appropriated. Inappropriate words cross swords.

My eyes sting with salty weeping. Salt from within.

Nelly and Bea
Go down to the sea
Then to the park
For a lark

Water off a leaf
's back
Belief

I'm sorry, I missed that. Sorry. I *am* sorry. Immortal immoral. Sun drenched reality.

What kind of dirt is that under the nails?

Why mock battle re-enactments? Are there not enough exactments? Mock mock.

And reading just puts ideas into one's head.

He came back a little to himself given the all clear.

It's not a book of stupid aphorisms.

Death is rotten. It is as rotten as the behaviour of politicians and publishers. Oh, don't be ridiculous.

When the goat guests applaud is it for the chef or the dish?

Your envy

Oh that she had never noticed that word before. Yeats later she did.

I am torn between. The serious is not taken lightly nor the light seriously. Russian pointlessness. The pretence of being seen, at any rate by oneself, to be at work. In a world of visual snows, virtual static. Deference or defence. Hurl-hurt. Hunted out of an unsafe haven.

The mire mine is quite empty. Shall I pummel pump the air with my clenched fist and elbow action at your winning streak? Fish streaking through the stream. Or, cutting the air with a racket, wondering what the air thinks about that shoulder swagger. What if there are no photos. So the flower closes up when it rains. Prickly heat rash. O 'tis a wilde gar*den* funny peopled. Tying trying so hard, echoing, hoping words have an indecipherable flat fate. Fish: I know little about it but the first and in my memory the only time I fished I caught two. Perch. Lake Thun. I was a child. I would like to know more about fish. Like Rick Stein. Accoutrements. It's cheap to make a heart with your fingers. —Yes, IT COSTS YOU NOTHING SO STOP WAVING YOUR FLAGS.

Alert. At every chance turn a dance.

At first reading Lispector's *The Besieged City* seemed claustrophobic. That seems to be the right word. On second reading, a good while later, not at all.

That morning Ir dressed in flared thigh-length plaid skirt, pleats? I'm not sure, I don't think so, off-white stocking tights, shoulder-length black hair, her usual white earmuffs., tasselled leather satchel, ?Docs. ?Lace-ups. Not in vain. He, at least, saw her, at the counter.

So they made flutter waves. Curious that café, unlike other cafés, they had not frequented it at the same time as each other before.

I don't know how to write that.

In the photo
A little French frog
Sat on a log
It isn't
It's a very low slab seat stone
She was on her own

She looked to the side
For somewhere to hide
I'll just have to show
'cause there's nowhere to go

Is that the best you can do? pouts dubious Nel
Yes, I'm so sorry, I'm so overwhelmed with French blue

I don't know how to write this.

"on a crumbling balustrade somewhere on the borderline of time" as Bruno Schulz writes in "Spring". What is it with balustrades? Supervielle, Ungaretti, Musil, to name three others. Broken down more often than not.

But the girls' eyes grow deeper
Flutterbyes

I know it is hot today but even so, flimsy hardly even thigh-length dress close to naked flower open. Stomp, no, stamp, shire hoofs.

R has been painting nails with her girls. Now it is raining. Apparition of the snails.

Maybe I can read a book but I cannot read you he was thinking, mouthing. He sank into himself on the terrace, nearer to her if they were reading the same book.

The ends of her loose black trouser legs frayed, hair loose. But in a photo standing, smart black, feet crossed, hair tied back. And I think a lighter colour. Portrait of a waif. Flower atop a stem.

Ah, what do I know? Very little about some many things. Staring into space stars in space faint glow

And all that that has passed
arriving invisibility
clambering
what you carry with within you
let us make giddy ourselves
that makes a way with it

Yes, I know about those cans of figs in syrup

To leave in peace or pieces

I tried to write stories as a child. Maybe I would manage a line or two, then I would look at the page expecting the words to materialize of their own accord. Today I look, or turn away from looking, at the dust in my house, wishing it away with the spider silk. I seem to think I can exercise just by looking at the exercise ropes, resistance bands, gymstick (if that is what they are called) stood in a corner. Once or twice a year I write a book or edit an issue of a review. If only they could distribute themselves just by being looked at, inside or outside their cartons. Sh' thinks I should paint and draw, but I can only make quick improvisatory marks.

Inhabit inhibit

I would like to know who first said coffee is a magical substance that turns "leave me alone or die" into "good morning, honey!"

Brow beaten into a twisted agenda
And they come again
flirting their trip
And turn to turn to
adressing your
notes to myself

An hotel cheap job
come flicker past
it must be written out
again and again
to satisfy laughter
gothic

O my half-broken down nose
Yes it was broken once at sport
With a broken vein that looks like not
What it looks like
O my forehead fencing scar not that either
O my weeping stinging eyewatered
Dew drops

Tears

YESTERDAY TODAY AND TOMORROW

Caricature has no h
Crayon on the paving
Little yelps behind the bench. Yelps swaying on the branches of the
    quince
A profound effect
Soft murmurs in the breeze
Phone talk
"The commander shall tremble at his own disorders"
Corking machine
The face is an experience
Perfume from the Gardens' wedding guests overwhelming the
    flowers'

INTERMEZZO

Gets who want to sell you the country's most popular burial plan grinning their early evening TV heads off don't fall off a ladder yet or fall asleep in the tub I should think so pure sans additives sunflowers for life

✼

    I would not play ball

I must write it out again and again for your laughter of
gothic extremities oh yes why shy away from not let us publish
rubbish

O fire, my splendid beauty
everything that you disturb
in our oftentimes vulgar land
it odes—what! that should be does—not travel well nor bodes well
escape me my lovely then silence

Displayed leg
the trial
comic is over

I do not know where my words have gone
Your words are true but but they aren't any use
I leave the lights on over
an explanation

Another glimpse
Are you having fun up there down there . . . ?

ANOTHER POEM FOR NELLY

Nel's little legs
On a walk on a walk
Listen to the bells
Don't talk don't talk
O how they beg they beg
Treading on egg-
Shells

Is that another really the best you can do? I'm so sorry

I am not at all sure I always recognize you it is you

So to another question
Who am I? Who are you?
You answer
There is nothing but a a
An a, surely?
No, a a
A a

WORDS FOR TORLEIV
Read at restaurant Lorry, Oslo, 2 September 2024

MY APOLOGIES that I cannot be with you in person to celebrate the life of Torleiv. Please accept these few words in my place.

It is with a heavy heart that I learn, from Ola, of the passing of Torleiv, a great and true friend and colleague from the time we first met, before his publishing and editing activities, when we both worked at Tanum in the 1970s, and continuing after my return to England. I first told the story of that episode in our lives in *Skal vi ta en runde til? Festskrift til Torleiv Grue, 7 mars 1998*.

It is with a lighter heart that I remember so fondly our times together, sometimes serious, sometimes hilarious, including his insistence on bringing me back to Oslo for your international poetry festival, in the face of opposition from the British Council, who, along with our Arts Council, have, unlike you in Norway, never really known what to do with its poets. I remember too Torleiv and Toril's patience with my, surely irritating, questions when I was grappling with translating *When the Robbers Came to Cardamom Town* at their summer house on Nesodden—well, that's my translation of the title, and what a battle it was with the Egner family to convince them of that. My home town of Lewes is not, in some respects, unlike Cardamom Town, so back here I would walk around pretending to be the characters in order to try to get the songs right. The Norwegian press took me to task for seemingly relegating Politimester Bastian to the status of Superintendent rather than Inspector but at the time I thought the song melody required that. Today I'm not so sure and think there was another way of handling that. Nevertheless, for years it has given me great pleasure to wander around my town, mouthing the words of Aunt Sophia: If only everybody was like me / it would be very good. / But no one is at all like me. / They don't do what they should.

But I digress. Here in Lewes I am raising with you a glass or two of Lysholm Linie Aquavit to the memory of a wonderful man, a true friend and colleague to myself and to many: Torleiv!

And if you will allow, I'd like to end these few words with a little sort of rhyming poem—does it also work in Norwegian?

Dear Torleiv Grue	Kjære Torleiv Grue
But for you	Men for deg
In this life	I dette livet
We can be sure	Kan vi være sikre på
Our poets would be fewer	Våre diktere ville vært færre

i.m. 7 March 1948 - 23 August 2024

*

Knocking a spider away
finding what is
is is
so much impinges
so many chordings
and short memory
little keys
away
a talk back
furious
distinctly
walking in godly unenclosed voices

travelling from the hillock
into oblivion
all quite quiet
and forgetting they are there
such elegance in her reading
(what is she reading?)
sipping her tea as I am
mistaken

SHAKESPEARE AND PROUST

Remembrance of Things Past is a brilliant title. *In Search of Lost Time* is soulless.

A LOST SISTER

"It is curious", A said, "when we look forward or long for some event in the future, or wish it over quickly, as if hurrying time when instead of slowing it down." "Yes", U said.

It's what I hear

Profound effect. You have taught me not to bother turning up my too long trousers.

*

LEBANON 17, 18 SEPTEMBER 2024
Eyeless Fingerless Waistless Legless

*

Hide. What part of speech?
An elephant calf between his or her mother's legs.

FROM STONE TO CLAY TO BUTTER

Discovering captivating early poems scattered throughout painter Celia Paul's memoir *Self-Portrait* (Cape, 2019) has set me to thinking about artists who also write poems. This is nothing new: from centuries ago Michelangelo's *Sonnets* easily comes to mind, in several translations, including that of Elizabeth Jennings (Carcanet, 2003). *Some Poems* by Paul Klee was nicely put into English by Anselm Hollo (Scorpion, 1962). Picasso too, who liked to put his hand to most everything. And doubtless, Celia Paul does not see herself as a poet on an equal footing as an artist, but some certainly do, David Jones, Blake, equally so or even more so. Three whose work I am most recently acquainted with are Monica Ferrando: her painting and philosophy essay, with Giorgio Agamben, translated from Italian, *The Unspeakable Girl: The Myth and Mystery of Kore* (Seagull, 2014), is her only book in English, though Barry Schwabsky has translated a suite of her poems, with drawings, in *Snow lit rev* 11; Lu Rose Cunningham, a graduate of Glasgow School of Art, who, amongst other, innovative, work, makes wonderfully complex and thoughtful drawings—drawing is not a lost art for her (Cunningham's Broken Sleep poetry book *Interval: House, Lover, Slippages* is reviewed in *PN Review* 270); and now Lily Petch, just graduated from The Slade with a material oriented installation for her degree show.

Dunlin Press, in Wivenhoe, is a publisher very much in favour of interactions between literature and art. In fact, Lily Petch's poetry début *From Stone to Clay to Butter* is text only, but is to a large extent drawn from a brick-coloured-cover book of texts, photos, diagrams, ancient and modern, displayed in an open case of reclaimed bricks at her degree show, apropos, but not only so, the origin of language: *The written unit, signs, gravemarkers and the left behind object*. Petch's description is "To pay close attention to the way in which we treat writing as a tool to preserve presence beyond the boundaries of the body. A tribute to the act of recording traces of ancestry by sign."

In *From Stone to Clay to Butter*: "Thoughts surrounding the invention of the written unit—born from a categorisation of surrounding objects and entities." And "First there was this large thing which bore a kind of substance you could eat.": that's tree and fruit. I do not think I can do justice quoting just a line or two: "The below surface feels infinite." Petch's writing is filled with knowledge, wisdom, discovery, mysteriousness, and it is, I believe, in defiance of a kind of matter-of-factness, magical and beautiful. This is most lovingly, even if heart-rendingly, embodied in a new poem Petch has written entitled "But What Is Forward Now All Is Dust", from a three-poem sequence "Daybreak", in *Snow lit rev* 14, which shadows motifs already to be found in *From Stone to Clay to Butter*:

> And the wind said, "try seeing the whole of history so far unravel itself".
> So we harnessed a tool and a sign and a tongue and shot our way off into the future.
>
> And she said in reply, "after destruction the forward motion to reparation must be warped—the linear path must be altered".
> So we broke it apart beneath our feet until the tool, sign, and tongue could no longer grasp its meaning.
>
> And after all this the soil said, "skin on skin is best".
> So we buried the broken fragments of some kind of meaning where skin could find no touch to linger.
>
> (But what is forward now all is dust?)

*

Sometimes I may do something that may not be so wrong.

Jesus, how you were fallen for if not necessity?

Necessity

To divest oneself of certain authors one might imagine one would want not to.

Things come to life, oops, light

If I bury my head in the sand
conducive conductive

Are you are you
lost for words
and ever after

Here I am not inspired
insipid vacant

Shame
What a shame
Yes yet there are
magical words they line up
queuecumbers
and give an impression of reality
for seriousness is not to be taken too lightly
nor the light too seriously—I wonder—
Russian pointlessness
pretence of being
seen to be a working of things

Bent back
Can I read?

You are abstracting the view
Clinging to a bench for dear life. Dear Life . . .

shadows lengths
a child scoots by on a pedalless bike
a laugh
contemplation

Now how can I expect meaning to stare
you in the face
Shall we go back
to what has been said:
Are you the wind that . . . ?
abiding aboding
because the clouds disperse
their breathing their breezing
rot

FINGER EXERCISES

My visionary vision is unusually blurred
But weary with involuntary salt weeping
You are so many, writhing in sand and air
You alternate
Where the waves, memory of my heart?

Geese arriving departing
Writing drum sticks and brushes
You are the poet whose work I like
You are not dross n drivel
Thank gggod

Whingeing a miracle
What other word is there for it
The history of uncertain things

I do not know sufficiently well or at all
So I am so to speak lost in the welter

O colours where my paper tigers are
Definitely more than one
I saw them aleap on their prey
Prayed all were there
They were of one stripe y'know

No longer amazed
What you think you can do, and do
You know the repercussion awaits
You in your and others' deserts and desserts—
Irrational thoughts and sighs

You see only to the end of a broken nose
Smutterings
That's right stick your feet up on the seat
In the train in the restaurant. Yes my dear
I'm not your dear

Open mouthed
Combat obscenities
May uncross
Salt on the wound
Open

A Sunday afternoon. Autumn
Like a child shuffling leaves
Like a child splashing puddles
Catching a ball and a breath
Or why the piano lid's locked

O dear, yes, again
Yes
I would listen to the news
In abeyance
Who does not hold their heads in their hands

A HILLY TOWN

It is a hilly town that seems to me to be a cross between Hrabal's Little Town Where Time Stood Still—it has a long established brewery, from the late seventeen hundreds, not to mention all the more recent, hm, craft brewhouses—and Egner's Cardamom Town, though it has not just one bakery shop but several, which some canine chorus or other seems to think it has the right to turn into barkeries, or rather their masters and mistresses do. We all like to complain about this or that, even though it's a pretty town and pretty much a peaceful one. Apropos that: ought not the Protestant bonfire night engage in a running battle up on the Downs with that Catholic town over to the west? Are things looking up? I can count close to twenty coffee shops or spots but I couldn't say I'd recommend them all. Coffee can be over-artisan, sour, or not artisan enough. Take your pick. One new, so delicate, aromatic, coffee house and roastery, with a pottery studio, also stocks books of a most uncommon sort and so must be applauded. After a long period of two or three traditional hotels being run into the ground—one no longer a hotel, one shuttered by an erstwhile local villain—a third has reopened under new ownership. It's been completely done over. The menus are good—one for the spacious restaurant, one for the barrooms. The service is good. The art works on the walls are kitsch. The sleeping rooms are, well, a bit overdone. There you are: one has to find something to complain about. I could go on but I won't. Mr Walser has written similar accounts about his cities and towns and his lakes and what have yous far more effectively than I can and I recommend they be read.

AS IT WERE

He sent her a message consisting entirely of emojis. A rosy cheeked smiley in the subject heading. A snowflake and a bunch of roses in the message itself. He had come across her in the coffee house, a little bit in the doldrums, but typing away anyway. The coffee house where an event was planned for the new year. Why anyone would want to break up with her was beyond him. Or had it been the other way round? It was not for him to be too inquisitive. If she wanted to speak she would. Yes, she confirms, all her writing is autobiography. That may be but it has an objectivity beyond subjectivity, if that makes sense.

LITERARY LETTER

You certainly confuse us. And how wrong you are about England. I do not say to whom this letter is addressed. Only several literary figures real or made up, no longer alive or alive. Silent or loquacious. If loquacious not silent. Figure that you wannabe philosophers. I dare say numbscull in reference to myself which is over-polite in deference to you, m'luds. You are slinging mud. Your differentiation, distinguishing in literary manners between intelligent man and witty woman is not acceptable. Oh, heavens, look out the window, it's pouring cats and dogs. Desk-bound. Your writing really really annoys me. You wear your learning in such a way you think you can explain everything that has passed and everything that is to come. But the present? Where is it? There is no presence. The hand grows heavy picking up the kettle to fill it. And a kind of hollow feeling in the stomach after eating quite wordinary mushrooms. There is hardly a doubt. Thinker. Stinker. Entering your intromittent organ into everythinking. Your expression of emphatic conclusions is really really annoying. No *An Answer*. Only vehement *The*. Is it possible I do not understand? Is it? Wet leaves of the passion flower glistening in the evening. And, No, it is most improbable that Sappho threw herself into the sea.

A SIMPLIFICATION

"Next year in Jerusalem" is the usual translation of the phrase, a sentence, recited by traditional Jews as the conclusion to the recitation of the Haggadah on Passover and the final service, Ne'ilah [closing], on Yom Kippur, followed by sounding the shofar, a ram's horn. It evokes the desire of certain Jewish believers to return from exile, often termed the diaspora, to Jerusalem when the Temple is rebuilt with the coming of the messiah, anointed warrior-leader. "Eyeless in Gaza" has its origin in Old Testament Judges: ". . . and put out his eyes, and brought him down to Gaza . . ." The phrase itself is Milton's in *Samson Agonistes*. Samson, in destroying the Temple, engineers his own death. And I say again: What then?   21 Oct. 2024

And again: Wet leaves of the passion flower glistening in the evening.

Lap it up. Speechless. Silence of the brain. Let me . . . think about that. The composition is a little tired. It has heard itself played so often. Do you know what you do? As it were.

INSIDE OUT

Changing bed linen is an amazing thing. Such freshness to go to sleep in. But it isn't easy. Struggling with the cover over the duvet, the duvet inside the cover, is a struggle, as I've already said, if you don't know the best way. Or do but can't be bothered, so sure your short cut will come out right. There are occasions, not looking forward to it, when one might not change the linen as often as one ought. That's not a good idea. But what a relief when it's done. When the cover is over so to speak. Exhaustion. Oh no, the cover is inside out. Oh well, best leave it like that. Blissful sleep. Just dreaming of a cover inside out. Why write about such an inconsequential thing as changing linen, whether it really is linen, or, in this case, Egyptian cotton? Why not? Burlock. What is it? It is made up from translating the Norwegian for velcro, *borrelås*: burdock lock. You know the story of velcro, don't you, made up of Fr. *velours* (velvet) and *crochet* (hook). Yes I do.

A DAMSON IN DISTRESS!

Alan Garner tells us that is what his grandson, shaking his head, pretending grief, sobbed on his sixth birthday, seeing a fruit lying squashed where it had fallen. Garner recounts the episode in a lecture he gave in Manchester and Cambridge, "Old Men's Trousers and the Making Strange of Things", reprinted in *Powsels and Thrums: A Tapestry of a Creative Life* (2024). Among other wisdoms the lecture shows up the difference between "translation" and "interpretation". "Powsels and Thrums"? Snippets of left-over cloth kept by handloom weavers for their own use. Stand alone pieces carrying a common thread. A couple of years ago only I began to read Garner's books, on the recommendation of my dear friend R, quickly to discover that two more close colleagues, Lewes T and Tokyo T have also garnered those books, some of which are terrifying. I, scaredy-cat.

SPICE BOX

CARDAMOM

In 1993 (corr. ed. 1994) my translation of Norway's best loved illustrated children's story, *Folk og røvere i Kardemomme by*, appeared under the title *When the Robbers Came to Cardamom Town*. It was no mean feat to convince the late author's family that nothing like "People and Robbers of Cardamon Town" would do in English, but I managed. After all, the French translation appeared under the title *Gens et Brigands de Pimentville*. Apparently, so I was told, the translator had convinced the family that cardamom was not sufficiently well known in France. True, cardamom is a feature of Scandinavian baking more so than elsewhere in Western Europe. But let us note cardamom's common use in coffee for people of The Middle East, of whom there are many in France. I rather think that the French translator had a different, even if also crass, point to make: "Piment d'Ville" (or "Piment d'Espelette", Espelette being a place where this variety of pepper has been cultivated) is a feature of Basque cooking. Not too far-fetched to move from "Piment d'Ville" to "Pimentville". Be that as it may, I feel deeply attached to cardamom, green cardamom, there is also a black cardamom, in my coffee or not.

CLOVE, CUMIN, CARAWAY, ETC

My first encounter with clove embedded in semi-hard or hard cheese was in Norway: *nøkkelost*, "key cheese". Often it also has cumin in. It dates from the seventeenth-century. This use of clove, and cumin, is believed to have originated in The Netherlands, where *kanterkaas*, "edge cheese" and *Kanternagelkaas*, "edge nail cheese" are documented in Friesland as far back as the fourteenth-century. I love it. When I do not have it I stick, and sprinkle, clove, and cumin or caraway, into and over mature cheddar, or other hard cheeses, with my toast. It is a bit different, of course. Schnips Schnoops Schnapps. What is that? It is what the great jazz violinist Hezekiah Leroy Gordon Stuff Smith liked to call akvavit, most often infused with caraway, also dill, fennel, cumin, etc, when he lived in Denmark, 1965–1967. Thereafter there was for a while the annual Stuff Smith Snoops Prize awarded to young musicians.

CORIANDER

Seeds, not leaf. Try them whole with chocolate, dark of course, or an orange, or both, blood orange if in season. Some give these seeds a bad press, with which I disagree.

LETTUCE LEAF BASIL, MOUNTAIN OR WINTER SAVORY, HISSOP

Yes, I know, Basil is an herb not a spice. If you say so. There is a variety I love that I used to be able to buy from an Italian delicatessen in Old Compton Street, Soho (the street with the store I buy coffee beans and cardamon pods from). The delicatessen is still there but it has not stocked this variety in donkeys' years. I remember it as cabbage leaf basil but it is better known as lettuce leaf. Large crinkled leaves. Lovely, pronounced yet delicate flavour. A search reveals that seeds are commercially available. I bought a packet. I sowed them in open pots outdoors. Mistake. Whenever seedlings appeared the next morning they were gone, gobbled by snails, I think, though I never did catch them in the act. Next year I had better cover them with a cloche. Savory, hissop, so good with cheeses, ewes' and goats'.

CINNAMON, GINGER

Indispensible. Warming. The one dried the other fresh, every time.

MORE TOTAL NONSENSE

Halloween
Is in-between
The 30th and the 1st
Which means it must Bea
On the 31st
And that's not the worst
It's cursed

But what does that mean? Bea said inquiringly
Mean? Mean?
Do you not know it does not mean
It just is
I see, Bea said thoughtfully, I thought it might mean
Bean, or has been

What if it does, said the Cheddar cat
Cheshire, Cheshire
Oh, alright, Caerphilly

WHAT PLACE IS

One reaction to poets preoccupied with place, external place, is to propose that for the poem itself place resides only in the poem. To say otherwise is hogwash because the poem can only *walk about talk about* external place. Internal place is the poem itself. What am I saying? Home? Abstraction? Yet, I have to ask myself how objective am I being? Might such a reaction arise from some perceived ancestral rootlessness? A rootless cosmopolitanism that certain poets who believe themselves firmly rooted like to denigrate? This is or I am going nowhere. Copping out of a meinfeld of *Centaurea cyanus*.

LECTURE

As this book draws in to its closing pages I ask myself what I have written over the several years it has been in progress. There are times when I have said what I wanted to say. There are other times I have not clearly understood myself or I have taken a risk. That's all right. I leave it to the reader who hopefully will do some of my thinking for me and make necessary adjustments, which may differ, each according to his or her own. There are also things I have not said, or I have said them elsewhere with the temptation but not the wish to say them again. I am reminded of Oscar Brown Jr's song: "Signifyin' Monkey / Stay up in your tree / You're always lyin' and signifyin' / But you better not monkey with me." I heard him in a nightspot, mid-1960s, with the Dudley Moore Trio. Why is this book 112 pages, including beginning and end papers? Usually my books are multiples of 32, sometimes, like here, with another 16. That way there is no wastage at the printer. One might say "the form and the content" of my books is ordered in that way. Odd? Even? As good as any other.

There are moments of gravity here and moments of levity. There are times I have drawn on observations, utterances and activities, of strangers, acquaintances, dear friends, and their children. I hope they may forgive me where forgiveness would be welcomed.

The World. We live in times terrible for many. Oh, right, then, nothing has changed. The Word. There are times when I am as outspoken as I feel I can be. There are, though, many times when I can only, so to speak, allude, infer. When it seems I must be oblique. That's me. There, again, I must ask the reader to do some work. I have scant religious knowledge but I wonder if somewhere in my bones lies a remnant of Kabbalah. And I have a tendancy, not so unusual, to want to open a book from the back. Hermeticism may not be quite as outlandish as Paul Celan thought. In deference to him, let alone myself, I shall say, I do not know for sure. What I do believe I know is that the so-called hermetic poets of Italy were nothing of the sort. There is nothing hermetic about a Giuseppe Ungaretti poem, unless hermetic is to mean embodied, not encrypted (paradox: in freedom secrets there are). Or, if there is, it is beyond me.

A piece "A View from the Kingdom" was folder-printed with a tiny 1981 pamphlet *A White Mess*. The piece was not included with reprints of the poem. This is as good an occasion as any. It is amended, with redactions, because the original context, which assimilated a 1963 painting *The Message to the White Man* by Czech painter, poet, psychiatrist, Václav Pinkava, and mentions of an English poet and an American poet concerning usefulness and irony, is not the same:

A White Mess. Social politics, sexual comedy, literary psychology, melting ice cap, a critical, religious (here I wrote negligious) mass.

"Absolutely not hermetic." Celan's transparent enjoining dismissed by an editor." I would like to understand and to be understood. I may not manage it one way or the other. Sometimes I write about what I do not understand. Meaning and reference are another matter. The reader has as much to work on as the writer (with rare exception and then annotation is in order).

What the reader does not have is source, which is just as well because source is a distraction. There is one thing more, impulse. It is possible to leave a line whose meaning in unclear. Fitting. I would like to know what happens. Then, whether or not I invent, I discover. I would not object to the word research. And progress is positive. I am not interested in damaging anything. I would say something like I discovered my politics (I found myself) in a straw.

The most useful poem gets restricted. Apparently it has no authority in the community so it is difficult to appropriate. I can see how resentment might follow ignorance. This useful poem is, rather than has, a moral imperative. It neither asserts nor demands. I would like to suggest a synthetic example: insisting on not following the instructions printed on a packet, sooner or later there is likely to be a mess. Saying a poem in useless I would not have a leg to stand on. With the compliment returned I go for a walk.

A poem is composed. It can hardly be anything else. It uses and sometimes alters a language appearing, at the moment it is used, like a set piece, head in the clouds. Conversation does this too. All the moments in the life of the language correspond to all the moments it is used. Style in a poem and a conversation differs —distinct facilities in understanding. Like anything else a poem tells the truth. I cannot stand unimaginative lies. I try not to be cowed by the joker who yells What truth! I might be amused by a true jest.

So, what exactly is all that alluding, inferring, obliquity? Well, you see, it is not exactly that at all. The poem is made, a balancing act, of sourcing. The objective sourcing is made up of words and their accoutrements and the subjective sourcing is made up of experiences and feelings and those sorts of things. So the poem is not its sources, which are at best not to be weighted heavily or lightly one side or the other. The poem is a newborn thing. If it means it means other than its mater and pater. If I were a philosopher or a philologist I might know better how to express these things (these after-the-work-is-done rationalizations). Or not, as the grammatical case may be.

POEM

O God, thou knowest. What? Where your tongue lies. In what
    sense lies? In the grammatical sense. I do not understand
    you. Then there are two of us.
Mysteries. Crazy knots. Suffocating, though not literally thank you
    very much, in a too-warm jumper.
Are you in love? Yes, I am.
It is a leopard, a Leopardi, a Leonardo, a leap.
A leap backwards or forwards?
What a question! One only a leopard can answer.

POEM

to Roger Giroux

Are you in love?
Yes, I am.
ppppoem, a struggle but at last I have got it out, hm, I think so
But who knows in the silent silex the iron irony
Do you misslove?
Mislove has one s
No, I do mean misslove
Miss, yes, I miss
Spring
Birch has the greenest leaf
Loki is the thief
Fall
Gently stew rhubarb with vanilla pod elderflower ginger a little
    cold pressed virgin olive oil honey for my love my love
You are happy with the nightmare, No, it is a daydream of mine.
The chefs are so pleased with themselves.
Breaking. Broken. Nov. 6th. It's ok. It's just a scene in a B-movie.
It is in the unnature of things that words turn on their heads.
Then you may while away time, brush the teeth of the crocodile.
God alone knows.
In a silent tongue of thought. In-worn double-flowers.
I catch myself looking and listening within an expression that is
    not mine but yours, complete with your features. It should
    be uncanny but it is not. I would say Thank you.

"A bird, as it flies,"

Where are our Sing Songs?

O, Sappho, you are so fragmented
yet not nearly so

> "AS FOR THE EXILES
> I think they had
> never found you,
> Peace, more difficult
> to endure!"

"This naïve and tentative God had no clue."

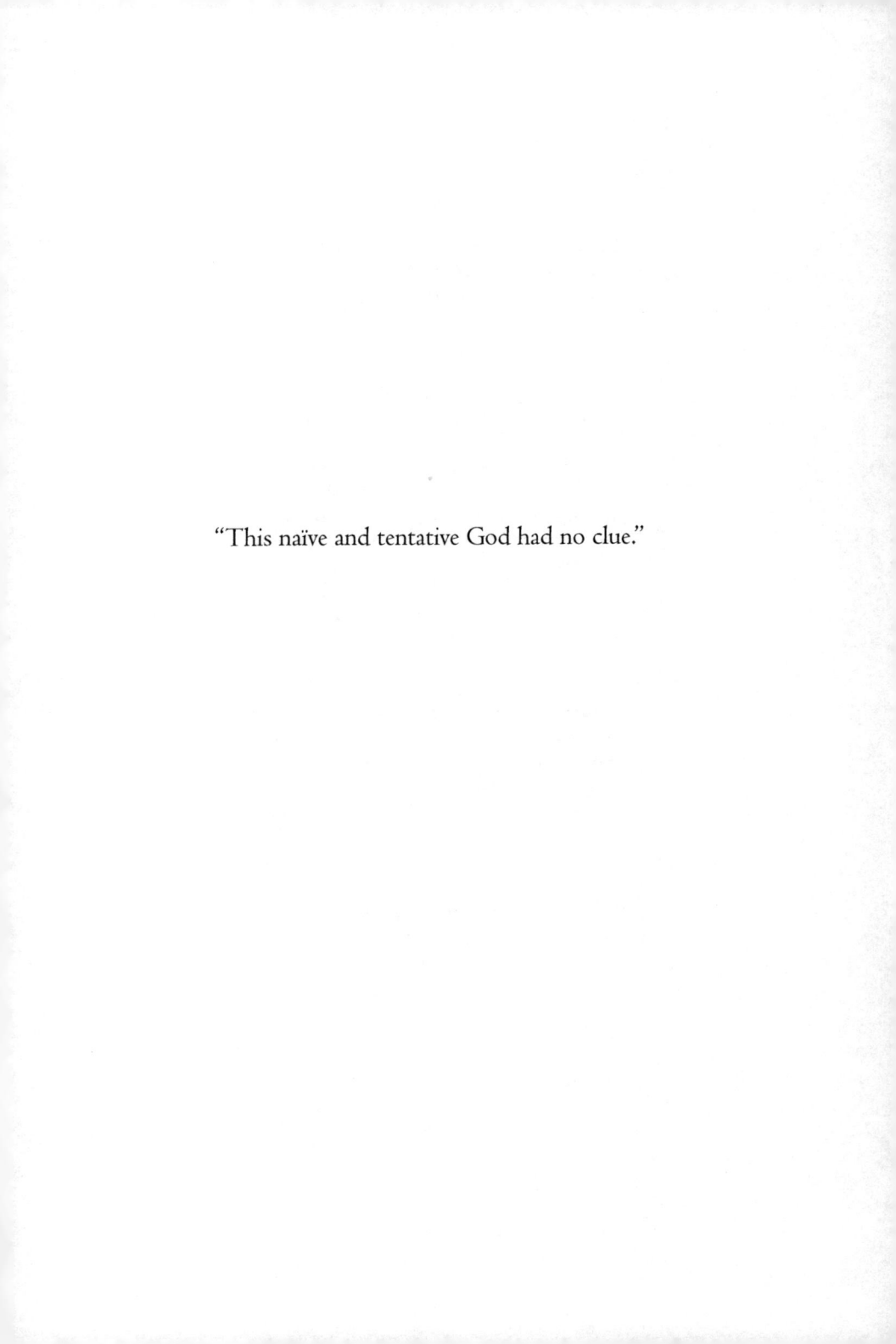

> By helping you, perhaps I was trying to lift up my life a trifle. Heaven knows anyone's life can stand a little of that.
> —E. B. White, *Charlotte's Web*

> The cat at play, the hauling beaver, the industrial ant, have no god in that sense. It would be truer to say that they 'are god' (but you had better be careful how and where you say it and what you mean by it); they are luckier than ourselves, they do not have to 'collaborate with God in the making'. They excel the House of Stuart, for if they can do no wrong, neither can they do any right —no wonder cats can look at kings. It must be a fine life, but it is definitely not the life of the artist.
> —David Jones, "Art and Democracy"
> *Epoch and Artist*

> But right up to the last there is hope of life. Fears that there's nothing to be afraid of anymore. This very evening you'll be sharing your dinner-table with Abraham. But God knows I'd rather not eat. I've sent death packing . . . by wanting to live.
> —Bohumil Hrabal, *Pirouettes on a Postage Stamp*

> Cualquier que se la causa que yo tenga que defender ante Dios más allá de la muerte, tengo un defensor: Dios.
> —César Vallejo, *Contra el secreto profesional*
> *(libro de pensamientos)*

> Oh Gott, oh Gott, oh Gott, schon wieder ist einer tot!
> —Robert Musil, *Auftakt zum Zodiakus*

COVER PHOTO
A Bird of Prayer, 2023, by the Author

THE DANCE
first appeared in *Snow lit rev* 10, spring 2022

Quotations from José Saramago, *Manual of Painting
& Calligraphy: A Novel*, trans. Giovanni Pontiero

POETRY
first appeared as a review in *PN Review* 249
September–October 2019 and incorporates a
piece in *Antonyms Anew: Barbs & Loves*, 2016

MOSAIC
first appeared as a review in *PN Review* 246
March–April 2019, lightly altered here

The first quotation from Mandelstam is in the translation
by Jamey Gambrell in Marina Tsvetaeva, *Earthly Signs*

The quotation from Mandelstam's "The Noise of Time"
is in the translation by Clarence Brown

diesen Singsang voll Unverstand is a quotation from
Ingeborg Bachmann's story „Ein Schritt nach Gomorrha"

CLARICE LISPECTOR
A short version appeared in "Letters to the Editor"
in *PN Review* 268, November–December 2022

"crude joke"? - see Judith Schalansky, "Valais Alps:
Guericke's Unicorn" in her *An Inventory of Losses*

The procatinator is pictured in
Antonyms Anew: Barbs & Loves, 2016

"But it *is* a mistake . . ." is a quotation from
Yasunari Kawabata, *The Sound of the Mountain* in
the translation by Edward G. Seidensticker

Metamir - see Primo Levi, *The Mirror Maker*

The quotation from Bruno Schluz's "Spring"
is in the translation by Madeline G. Levine

"Yes, I know about those cans of figs in syrup" is a
response to a passage in Celia Paul, *Letters to Gwen John*

"The commander shall tremble at his own disorders"
defers to a sentence by Witold Gombrowicz, somewhere

WORDS FOR TORLEIV
"the story of that episode": "Fra det moderne norges aandsliv"
in English but for the title reprinted in *Poems &*, 2012

A LOST SISTER
A is not exactly Anthony, U is not exactly You, but could be
Robert Musil's siblings Agathe, Ulrich in *The Man Without Qualities*
[adulterine *Agathe: or, The Forgotten Sister*, NYRB, is severely deprecated]

FROM STONE TO CLAY TO BUTTER
first appeared as a review in *PN Review* 280, January–February 2025

A HILLY TOWN
ref. Thorbjørn Egner, *When the Robbers Came to Cardamom Town*, see preceding
"Words for Torleiv"; also ref. Hrabal see "What Is Wrong with This Town"

LITERARY LETTER
I suppose I should say to whom this letter is addressed; it is a critique
of Hugo von Hofmannsthal and his fictional Lord Chandos, and more
so of Pascal Quignard, whose translators, not unusually, usually do not
know when to write "he" & "she" and when to write "him" & "her"
and yet occasionally they do get it right, which begs the question . . .
As for Sappho: "The tale about the Leucadian cliffs is seldom
taken seriously nowadays."—Barnard, see *Sappho* fol.

POEM
"A bird, as it flies," is a quotation from Roger Giroux in *Time and the Tree*
repr. in AB's *Translations* - the "yours" of the preceding lines is not Giroux

"AS FOR THE EXILES . . ."
Mary Barnard, *Sappho*, in the most fitting translation

"This naïve and tentative God . . ." is a quotation from "God's Dream" by
Qian Zhongshu in *Humans, Beasts, and Ghosts: Stories and Essays*, ed. C. G. Reah

The quotation from Bohumil Hrabal is in the translation by David Short

have you noticed how when cracking nuts bits of shells fly all over the place